THE BEST-EVER BOOK OF
ITALIAN COOKING

THE BEST-EVER BOOK OF
ITALIAN COOKING

THE AUTHENTIC TASTE OF ITALY: 130 CLASSIC AND REGIONAL RECIPES SHOWN IN 270 STUNNING PHOTOGRAPHS

Edited by Gabriella Rossi

HERMES HOUSE

This edition is published by Hermes House,
an imprint of Anness Publishing Ltd,
Blaby Road, Wigston, Leicestershire LE18 4SE

info@anness.com

Web: www.hermeshouse.com;
www.annesspublishing.com

If you like the images in this book and would like
to investigate using them for publishing, promotions
or advertising, please visit our website
www.practicalpictures.com for more information.

Publisher: Joanna Lorenz
Editors: Elizabeth Young, Anne Hildyard
Designer: Ian Sandom
Cover Designer: Sarah Rock
Editorial Reader: Barbara Toft
Index: Helen Snaith
Production Controller: Wendy Lawson
Additional Recipes: Pepita Aris, Alex Barker, Jacqueline
Clark, Joanna Farrow, Christine Ingram, Becky Johnson,
Jane Milton, Jennie Shapter, Marlena Spieler, Linda Tubby
Photographers: Tim Auty, Martin Brigdale, Nicky
Dowey, Gus Filgate, Michelle Garrett, Amanda
Heywood, William Lingwood, Craig Robertson,
Simon Smith
Authors: Alex Barker, Angela Boggiano, Carla Capalbo,
Maxine Clark, Matthew Drennan, Brian Glover, Valentina
Harris, Sara Lewis, Kate Whiteman, Jenny White,
Jenni Wright

© Anness Publishing Ltd 2012

Main cover image shows *Ravioli in the pesaro style*
– for the recipe, see page 46–7

ETHICAL TRADING POLICY

At Anness Publishing we believe that business should
be conducted in an ethical and ecologically sustainable
way, with respect for the environment and a proper
regard to the replacement of the natural resources
we employ.

As a publisher, we use a lot of wood pulp in high-
quality paper for printing, and that wood commonly
comes from spruce trees. We are therefore currently
growing more than 750,000 trees in three Scottish
forest plantations: Berrymoss (130 hectares/320 acres),
West Touxhill (125 hectares/305 acres) and Deveron
Forest (75 hectares/185 acres). The forests we manage
contain more than 3.5 times the number of trees
employed each year in making paper for the books
we manufacture.

Because of this ongoing ecological investment
programme, you, as our customer, can have the pleasure
and reassurance of knowing that a tree is being
cultivated on your behalf to naturally replace the
materials used to make the book you are holding.

Our forestry programme is run in accordance with
the UK Woodland Assurance Scheme (UKWAS) and will
be certified by the internationally recognized Forest
Stewardship Council (FSC). The FSC is a non-
government organization dedicated to promoting
responsible management of the world's forests.
Certification ensures forests are managed in an
environmentally sustainable and socially responsible
way. For further information about this scheme, go to
www.annesspublishing.com/trees

PUBLISHER'S NOTE

Although the advice and information in this book are
believed to be accurate and true at the time of going to
press, neither the authors nor the publisher can accept
any legal responsibility or liability for any errors or
omissions that may be made nor for any inaccuracies
nor for any harm or injury that comes about from
following instructions or advice in this book.

NOTES

For all recipes, quantities are given in both
metric and imperial measures and, where
appropriate, in standard cups and spoons.
Follow one set of measures, but not a mixture,
because they are not interchangeable.
Standard spoon and cup measures are level.
1 tsp = 5ml, 1 tbsp = 15ml, 1 cup = 250ml/8fl oz.

Australian standard tablespoons are 20ml.
Australian readers should use 3 tsp in place of
1 tbsp for measuring small quantities.

American pints are 16fl oz/2 cups. American
readers should use 20fl oz/2.5 cups in place of
1 pint when measuring liquids.

Electric oven temperatures in this book are for
conventional ovens. When using a fan oven, the
temperature will probably need to be reduced by
about 10–20°C/20–40°F. Since ovens vary, you
should check with your manufacturer's
instruction book for guidance.

The nutritional analysis given for each recipe is
calculated per portion (i.e. serving or item),
unless otherwise stated. If the recipe gives a
range, such as Serves 4–6, then the nutritional
analysis will be for the smaller portion size, i.e.
6 servings. Measurements for sodium do not
include salt added to taste.

Medium (US large) eggs are used unless
otherwise stated.

Contents

Introduction

Italians are passionate about their cuisine and always enjoy spending time preparing, cooking and eating meals with family and friends. Food is one of their greatest pleasures and Italians are fortunate to be able to enjoy many regional variations of the dishes they eat.

A DIVERSE LANDSCAPE

Italian cooking reflects the fact that the country was only unified in 1861. Until then, each region produced its own characteristic cuisine, relying exclusively on ingredients that could be gathered, cultivated or reared locally. Nowadays of course, regional produce can easily be transported all over the country, but Italians still prefer to base their cooking on local ingredients, because they regard quality and freshness as more important than diversity and innovation. So, the most flavourful sun-ripened tomatoes, aubergines (eggplant) and (bell) peppers are still found in the south, the freshest seafood is available along the coast, and the finest hams come from the area where the pigs are raised.

La cucina italiana remains distinctly regional; northern Italian cooking, for example, incorporates ingredients that are simply never found in the recipes of Sicily and Naples, and vice versa. In the dairy-farming north, butter is used in place of the olive oil so prevalent in the south; bread and polenta are eaten instead of pasta. The only unifying feature is the insistence on high-quality ingredients.

Good food has always been essential to the Italian way of life. One of the oldest cooking cultures in the world, the cuisine dates back to the Ancient Greeks and perhaps even earlier.

A great deal of Italian food comes from *contadino*, or peasant, heritage – combining fresh ingredients with simple cooking techniques. Meats, fish and vegetables are flavoured with herbs and olive oil, and often grilled (broiled) or baked. Aromatic sauces can often be assembled in the time it takes pasta to boil.

BELOW: *Traditional meat roasts make a tasty family meal.*

ABOVE: *The coastal areas of Italy provide a good supply of all kinds of seafood.*

ABOVE: *Pasta is a nutritious staple that can be formed into a variety of shapes.*

ABOVE: *Olives and cured meats are a popular antipasto dish.*

ITALIAN FOOD TODAY

The essence of Italian cooking today is simplicity. The Italian way of cooking fish is most often grilled (broiled) over hot coals, then served with nothing more than a splash of extra virgin olive oil, a wedge of lemon and freshly ground black pepper. Recipes such as carpaccio di tonno, in which the fish is so succulent raw that cooking seems unnecessary, and grigliata di calamari, squid grilled with chillies, are typical.

Italians learn to appreciate good food when they are young children, and eating is one of the major pleasures of the day. The first course, or antipasto, is a unique feature.

In restaurants, this can be a vast array of different dishes, both hot and cold, from which diners can choose as few or as many as they wish. At home it is more likely to be a slice or two of salame or prosciutto crudo with fresh figs or melon, if these are in season.

The variety of Italian ingredients available at supermarkets and delicatessens will inspire you to concoct any number of flavourful meals, from an uncomplicated dish of pasta to a full-blown four-course dinner. A plate of antipasto followed by pasta, or risotto flavoured with seasonal ingredients, then by grilled meat or fish and finally local cheese and fruit, makes a veritable feast.

USING THIS BOOK

Perfect for lovers of wholesome Italian food, this book will increase the repertoire of any cook. The book features a superb collection of 130 authentic recipes, featuring a variety of dishes from around Italy, from regional specialities to popular modern classics, all of which have been tested to ensure perfect results. Most of the recipes are intended for a family of four people, but the quantities can easily be halved to serve two, or doubled for eight. At the end of the book, there is a guide to traditional Italian produce, with tips for storing, preparing, and cooking with them.

Soups and antipasti

Antipasto means 'before the meal',

and no respectable Italian meal would

start without it. The recipes in this

chapter are typical of antipasti –

appetizing, light and tasty. Delicious

soups can be made in no time at all; clear

broths and delicate puréed soups are

served as a light first course, while more

substantial soups, such as minestrone,

can be a meal in themselves.

Fresh tomato soup

Intensely flavoured sun-ripened tomatoes need little embellishment in this fresh-tasting dish. On a hot day, this Italian favourite is just as good served chilled.

SERVES 6

1.3–1.6kg/3–3¹/₂lb ripe tomatoes
400ml/14fl oz/1²/₃ cups chicken or vegetable stock
45ml/3 tbsp sun-dried tomato paste
30–45ml/2–3 tbsp balsamic vinegar
10–15ml/2–3 tsp caster (superfine) sugar
small handful of basil leaves, plus extra to garnish
salt and ground black pepper
toasted cheese croûtes and crème fraîche, to serve

1 Plunge the tomatoes into boiling water for 30 seconds, then refresh in cold water. Peel away the skins and quarter the tomatoes. Put them in a large pan and pour over the chicken or vegetable stock. Bring just to the boil, reduce the heat, cover and simmer the mixture gently for 10 minutes until the tomatoes are pulpy.

2 Stir in the tomato paste, vinegar, sugar and basil. Season with salt and pepper, then cook gently, stirring, for 2 minutes. Process the soup in a blender or food processor, then return to the pan and reheat gently.

3 Serve in bowls, topped with one or two toasted cheese croûtes and a spoonful of crème fraîche, garnished with basil leaves.

Nutritional information per portion: Energy 49kcal/210kJ; Protein 1.9g; Carbohydrate 9.5g, of which sugars 9.5g; Fat 0.7g, of which saturates 0.2g; Cholesterol 0mg; Calcium 19mg; Fibre 2.4g; Sodium 38mg.

Broccoli soup with garlic toast

This recipe originates from Rome. For the best colour, use the freshest broccoli you can find and a good quality Parmesan cheese, such as Parmigiano-Reggiano.

SERVES 6

675g/1¹/₂lb broccoli spears
1.75 litres/3 pints/7¹/₂ cups chicken
    or vegetable stock
salt and ground black pepper
30ml/2 tbsp fresh lemon juice
freshly grated Parmesan cheese
    (optional), to serve

FOR THE GARLIC TOAST

6 slices white bread
1 large garlic clove, halved

1 Using a small sharp knife, peel the broccoli stems, starting from the base of the stalks and pulling gently up towards the florets. (The peel comes off very easily.) Chop the broccoli into small chunks.

2 Bring the stock to the boil in a large pan. Add the chopped broccoli and simmer for 20 minutes, or until soft.

3 Purée about half of the soup in a blender or food processor and then mix into the rest of the soup. Season with salt, pepper and lemon juice.

4 Just before serving, reheat the soup to just below boiling point. Toast the bread, rub with garlic and cut into quarters. Place 3 or 4 pieces of toast in the base of each soup plate. Ladle on the soup. Serve immediately, with grated Parmesan cheese, if using.

Nutritional information per portion: Energy 98kcal/413kJ; Protein 7.2g; Carbohydrate 14.6g, of which sugars 2.4g; Fat 1.5g, of which saturates 0.2g; Cholesterol 0mg; Calcium 91mg; Fibre 3.4g; Sodium 139mg.

Wild mushroom soup

Dried porcini have an intense taste, so only a small quantity is needed. The beef stock may seem unusual in a vegetable soup, but it helps to strengthen the earthy flavour of the mushrooms.

SERVES 4

25g/1oz/2 cups dried porcini mushrooms
30ml/2 tbsp olive oil
15g/¹/₂ oz/1 tbsp butter
2 leeks, thinly sliced
2 shallots, roughly chopped
1 garlic clove, roughly chopped
225g/8oz/3 cups fresh wild
    mushrooms, sliced
1.2 litres/2 pints/5 cups beef stock
2.5ml/¹/₂ tsp dried thyme
salt and ground black pepper
150ml/¹/₄ pint/²/₃ cup double
    (heavy) cream
fresh thyme sprigs, to garnish

1 Put the dried porcini in a bowl, add 250ml/8fl oz/1 cup warm water and leave to soak for 20–30 minutes. Lift out of the liquid and squeeze over the bowl to remove as much of the liquid as possible. Strain all the liquid and reserve to use later. Finely chop the porcini.

2 Heat the oil and butter in a large pan until foaming. Add the leeks, shallots and garlic and cook gently for about 5 minutes, stirring frequently, until softened.

3 Add the fresh mushrooms to the pan. Stir over medium heat for a few minutes until they begin to soften. Pour in the stock and bring to the boil. Add the porcini, soaking liquid, dried thyme and salt and pepper. Simmer gently for 30 minutes.

4 Pour about three-quarters of the soup into a blender or processor and process until smooth. Return to the soup in the pan, stir in the cream and heat through. Season. Serve hot, garnished with thyme sprigs.

Nutritional information per portion: Energy 149kcal/618kJ; Protein 3.1g; Carbohydrate 9g, of which sugars 0.5g; Fat 11.4g, of which saturates 6.9g; Cholesterol 28mg; Calcium 25mg; Fibre 1.5g; Sodium 79mg.

Aubergine soup with mozzarella and gremolata

Gremolata, a classic Italian mixture of garlic, lemon and parsley, adds a flourish of freshness to the rich and creamy texture of this tasty aubergine soup.

SERVES 6

30ml/2 tbsp olive oil

2 shallots, chopped

2 garlic cloves, chopped

1kg/2¼lb aubergines (eggplant), chopped

1 litre/1¾ pints/4 cups chicken stock

150ml/¼ pint/⅔ cup double (heavy) cream

30ml/2 tbsp chopped fresh parsley

175g/6oz buffalo mozzarella, thinly sliced

salt and ground black pepper

FOR THE GREMOLATA

2 garlic cloves, finely chopped

grated rind of 2 lemons

15ml/1 tbsp chopped fresh parsley

1 Heat the oil in a large pan and add the shallots and garlic. Cook for 4–5 minutes, until softened. Add the aubergines and cook for about 25 minutes, stirring occasionally, until they are very soft and browned.

2 Pour in the chicken stock and cook for about 5 minutes. Leave the soup to cool slightly.

3 Purée the soup in a food processor or blender until smooth. Return to the rinsed-out pan, and season. Add the cream and parsley, and bring to the boil.

4 Mix the ingredients for the gremolata. Ladle the soup into bowls and lay the mozzarella on top. Sprinkle with gremolata and serve.

Nutritional information per portion: Energy261kcal/1079kJ; Protein 7.5g; Carbohydrate 4.9g, of which sugars 4.3g; Fat 23.7g, of which saturates 13.1g; Cholesterol 51mg; Calcium 137mg; Fibre 3.5g; Sodium 124mg.

Broad bean, mangetout and spinach minestrone

The classic, wintry Italian minestrone soup takes on a summer-fresh image in this light recipe. Any small pasta shapes can be used instead of the spaghettini if you prefer.

SERVES 6

30ml/2 tbsp olive oil

2 onions, finely chopped

2 garlic cloves, finely chopped

2 carrots, very finely chopped

1 celery stick, very finely chopped

1.27 litres/2^1/$_4$ pints/5^2/$_3$ cups boiling water

450g/1lb shelled fresh broad (fava) beans

225g/8oz mangetouts (snow peas), cut into
  fine strips

3 tomatoes, peeled and chopped

5ml/1 tsp tomato paste

50g/2oz spaghettini, broken into
  4cm/1^1/$_2$in lengths

225g/8oz baby spinach

30ml/2 tbsp chopped fresh parsley

handful of fresh basil leaves, plus extra, to garnish

salt and ground black pepper

freshly grated Parmesan cheese, to serve, optional

1 Heat the oil in a pan and add the onions and garlic. Cook for 4–5 minutes, until softened. Add the carrots and celery, and cook for 2–3 minutes. Add the boiling water and simmer for 15 minutes, until the vegetables are tender.

2 Cook the broad beans in boiling salted water for 4–5 minutes. Remove with a slotted spoon, refresh under cold water and set aside.

3 Bring the pan of water back to the boil, add the mangetouts and cook for 1 minute until just tender. Drain, then refresh under cold water and set aside.

4 Add the tomatoes and the tomato paste to the soup. Cook for 1 minute. Purée two or three large ladlefuls of the soup and a quarter of the broad beans in a food processor or blender until smooth. Set aside.

5 Add the spaghettini to the remaining soup and cook for 6–8 minutes, until tender. Stir in the puréed soup and spinach and cook for 2–3 minutes. Add the rest of the broad beans, the mangetouts and parsley, and season well. When you are ready to serve the soup, stir in the basil leaves and ladle the soup into cups or bowls and garnish with sprigs of basil. Serve with grated Parmesan, if using.

Nutritional information per portion: Energy 201kcal/839kJ; Protein 8.1g; Carbohydrate 18.1g, of which sugars 7.8g; Fat 11.2g, of which saturates 3.4g; Cholesterol 10mg; Calcium 170mg; Fibre 3g; Sodium 138mg.

Onion soup

This warming winter soup, made with pancetta and onions, comes from Umbria, where it may be thickened with beaten eggs and grated Parmesan cheese. It is served over hot toasted croûtes.

SERVES 4

115g/4oz pancetta rashers (strips), any
   rinds removed, roughly chopped
30ml/2 tbsp olive oil
15g/¹/₂ oz/1 tbsp butter
675g/1¹/₂lb onions, thinly sliced
10ml/2 tsp sugar
about 1.2 litres/2 pints/5 cups
   chicken stock
350g/12oz ripe Italian plum tomatoes,
   peeled and roughly chopped
a few basil leaves, shredded
salt and ground black pepper
freshly grated Parmesan cheese, to serve

1 Put the pancetta in a large pan and heat gently, stirring, until the fat runs. Increase the heat to medium, add the oil, butter, onions and sugar.

2 Half-cover the pan and cook the onions gently for about 20 minutes until golden. Stir frequently and lower the heat if necessary.

3 Add the stock, tomatoes and salt and pepper and bring to the boil, stirring. Lower the heat, half-cover the pan and simmer, stirring occasionally, for about 30 minutes. If the soup is too thick, add a little more stock or water.

4 Just before serving, stir in most of the basil and taste for seasoning. Serve hot, garnished with the remaining shredded basil and the Parmesan.

Nutritional information per portion: Energy 273kcal/1136kJ; Protein 9g; Carbohydrate 19g, of which sugars 5g; Fat 6g, of which saturates 6g; Cholesterol 30mg; Calcium 56mg; Fibre 3.7g; Sodium 1125mg.

Cream of courgette soup

This soup is prized for its delicate colour, rich and creamy texture and subtle taste. If you prefer a more pronounced cheese flavour, use Gorgonzola instead of Dolcelatte.

SERVES 4–6

30ml/2 tbsp olive oil
15g/¹/₂oz/1 tbsp butter
1 medium onion, roughly chopped
900g/2lb courgettes (zucchini), trimmed
    and sliced
5ml/1 tsp dried oregano
about 600ml/1 pint/2¹/₂ cups vegetable
    or chicken stock
115g/4oz Dolcelatte cheese, rind
    removed, diced
300ml/¹/₂ pint/1¹/₄ cups single
    (light) cream
salt and ground black pepper
fresh oregano and extra Dolcelatte,
    to garnish

1 Heat the oil and butter in a large pan until foaming. Add the onion and cook gently for about 5 minutes, stirring frequently, until softened but not brown. Add the courgettes and oregano, with salt and pepper to taste. Cook over medium heat for 10 minutes, stirring frequently.

2 Pour in the stock and bring to the boil, stirring. Lower the heat, half-cover the pan and simmer gently, stirring occasionally, for about 30 minutes. Stir in the diced Dolcelatte until melted.

3 Process the soup in a blender or food processor until smooth, then strain into a clean pan. Add two-thirds of the cream and stir over a low heat until hot, but not boiling. Check the consistency and add more stock if the soup is too thick. Taste for seasoning, then pour into heated bowls. Swirl in the remaining cream. Garnish with oregano and extra cheese and serve.

Nutritional information per portion: Energy 248kcal/1024kJ; Protein 8.5g; Carbohydrate 5.4g, of which sugars 4.8g; Fat 21.5g, of which saturates 11.7g; Cholesterol 47mg; Calcium 181mg; Fibre 1.6g; Sodium 266mg.

Ribollita

This is a classic rustic soup from the Tuscan region of Italy. It is made with a combination of bread and vegetables – for an authentic version, you should use cavolo nero cabbage.

SERVES 6

115g/4oz/generous ¹/₂ cup cannellini beans,
   soaked overnight and drained
8 garlic cloves, unpeeled
30ml/2 tbsp olive oil
6 celery sticks, chopped
3 carrots, chopped
2 onions, chopped

400g/14oz can plum tomatoes, drained
30ml/2 tbsp chopped fresh flat leaf parsley
grated rind and juice of 1 lemon
800g/1³/₄lb cavolo nero, sliced
1 day-old ciabatta loaf
salt and ground black pepper
olive oil, to serve

1 Put the beans in a pan and cover with fresh water. Bring to the boil and boil for 10 minutes. Drain again. Cover generously with fresh cold water and add six garlic cloves. Bring to the boil, cover and simmer for 45–60 minutes, until the beans are tender. (The cooking time varies according to how old the beans are.) Set the beans aside in their cooking liquid.

2 Heat the oil in a pan. Peel and chop the remaining garlic and add it to the pan with the chopped celery, carrots and onions. Cook over a gentle heat for 10 minutes, until they begin to soften.

3 Stir in the tomatoes, parsley, lemon rind and juice. Cover and simmer for 25 minutes. Add the sliced cavolo nero and half the cannellini beans, with enough of their cooking liquid to cover. Simmer for 30 minutes.

4 Meanwhile, process the remaining beans with a little of their remaining cooking liquid in a food processor or blender until just smooth. Add to the pan and pour in boiling water to thin the mixture to the consistency of a thick soup.

5 Remove the crust from the ciabatta and tear the bread into rough pieces, then stir them into the soup. Season well. This soup should be very thick, but you may need to add a little more boiling water as the consistency varies depending on the bread. Ladle the soup into bowls and drizzle over a little olive oil. Serve immediately.

Nutritional information per portion: Energy 104kcal/436kJ; Protein 5.7g; Carbohydrate 14.5g, of which sugars 6.9g; Fat 3g, of which saturates 0.5g; Cholesterol 0mg; Calcium 78mg; Fibre 5.9g; Sodium 218mg.

Sausage and borlotti bean soup with breadcrumbs

A satisfying soup, this recipe is based loosely on cassoulet. Sausages and Italian beans contribute richness and substance, and the soup is topped with golden breadcrumbs.

SERVES 6

250g/9oz/generous 1¼ cups borlotti beans, soaked overnight and drained

115g/4oz piece pancetta, finely chopped

6 sausages, thickly sliced

1 large onion, finely chopped

2 garlic cloves, chopped

2 carrots, finely diced

2 leeks, finely chopped

6 tomatoes, peeled, seeded and chopped

30ml/2 tbsp tomato paste

1.27 litres/2¼ pints/5²⁄₄ cups vegetable stock

175g/6oz spring greens (collards), roughly shredded

25g/1oz/2 tbsp butter

115g/4oz/2 cups fresh white breadcrumbs

50g/2oz/²⁄₃ cup freshly grated Parmesan cheese

salt and ground black pepper

1 Place the beans in a pan. Cover with plenty of cold water and bring to the boil, then boil for 10 minutes. Drain well.

2 Heat a large pan and dry-fry the pancetta until browned and the fat runs. Add the sausages and cook for 4–5 minutes, stirring occasionally, until beginning to brown. Add the onion and garlic and cook for 3–4 minutes until softened. Add the beans, carrots, leeks, tomatoes and tomato paste, then add the stock. Stir, bring to the boil and cover.

3 Simmer for about 1¼ hours or until the beans are tender, then stir in the spring greens and cook for 12–15 minutes more. Season well.

4 Meanwhile, melt the butter in a frying pan and fry the breadcrumbs for 4–5 minutes, stirring, until golden, then stir in the Parmesan.

5 Ladle the soup into six bowls. Sprinkle the fried breadcrumb mixture over each, then serve.

Nutritional information per portion: Energy 574kcal/2405kJ; Protein 29g; Carbohydrate 47.7g, of which sugars 10.2g; Fat 31g, of which saturates 12.5g; Cholesterol 75mg; Calcium 284mg; Fibre 10.7g; Sodium 1179mg.

Bocconcini with fennel and basil

These tiny balls of mozzarella are best when they are perfectly fresh. They should be milky and soft when you cut into them. Buy them from an Italian delicatessen or a good cheese shop.

SERVES 6

450g/1lb bocconcini mozzarella
45ml/3 tbsp extra virgin olive oil
5ml/1 tsp fennel seeds, lightly crushed
a small bunch of fresh basil leaves,
    roughly torn
salt and ground black pepper

1 Drain the bocconcini well and place in a bowl. Stir in the olive oil, fennel seeds and basil, and season with salt and pepper. Cover and chill for 1 hour.

2 Remove the bowl from the refrigerator and leave to stand for about 30 minutes before serving to allow the cheese to return to room temperature .

Nutritional information per portion: Energy 245kcal/1015kJ; Protein 14.2g; Carbohydrate 0.2g, of which sugars 0.2g; Fat 20.8g, of which saturates 11.1g; Cholesterol 44mg; Calcium 288mg; Fibre 0.4g; Sodium 299mg.

Panzanella salad

If sliced, juicy tomatoes layered with day-old bread sounds strange for a salad, don't be deceived – it is quite delicious. A popular Italian antipasto, this dish is ideal for serving as an appetizer.

SERVES 4–6

4 thick slices day-old bread, either white, brown or rye

1 small red onion, thinly sliced

450g/1lb ripe tomatoes, thinly sliced

115g/4oz mozzarella cheese, thinly sliced

5ml/1 tbsp fresh basil, shredded, or fresh marjoram

120ml/4fl oz/½ cup extra virgin olive oil

45ml/3 tbsp balsamic vinegar

juice of 1 small lemon

salt and ground black pepper

stoned (pitted) and sliced black olives or salted capers, to garnish

1 Dip the bread briefly in cold water, then carefully squeeze out the excess liquid. Arrange the bread in the base of a shallow salad bowl.

2 Soak the onion slices in cold water for about 10 minutes while you prepare the other ingredients. Drain and reserve.

3 Layer the tomatoes, cheese, onion, basil or marjoram, seasoning well in between each layer.

4 Sprinkle with oil, vinegar and lemon juice. Top with the olives or capers, cover with clear film (plastic wrap) and chill in the refrigerator for at least 2 hours or overnight.

Nutritional information per portion: Energy 237kcal/987kJ; Protein 6.3g; Carbohydrate 15.4g, of which sugars 3.5g; Fat 17.1g, of which saturates 4.5g; Cholesterol 11mg; Calcium 105mg; Fibre 1.3g; Sodium 213mg.

Stuffed roast peppers with pesto

Serve these succulent scallop- and pesto-filled sweet red peppers with Italian bread,
such as ciabatta or focaccia, to mop up the garlicky juices.

SERVES 4

4 red (bell) peppers
2 large garlic cloves, cut into thin slivers
60ml/4 tbsp olive oil
4 scallops, shelled
45ml/3 tbsp pesto
salt and ground black pepper
freshly grated Parmesan cheese,
  to serve
salad leaves and fresh basil sprigs,
  to garnish

1 Preheat the oven to 180°C/350°F/Gas 4. Cut the peppers in half lengthways, through their stalks. Scrape out and discard the cores and seeds. Wash the pepper shells and pat dry.

2 Put the peppers, cut side up, in an oiled roasting pan. Divide the garlic equally among them and sprinkle with salt and pepper. Spoon the oil into the peppers, then roast for 40 minutes.

3 Cut each of the scallops in half to make two flat discs. Remove the peppers from the oven and place a scallop half in each pepper half. Top with pesto. Return to the oven and roast for 10 minutes more. Transfer to serving plates, sprinkle with grated Parmesan and garnish with salad leaves and basil sprigs.

Nutritional information per portion: Energy 325kcal/ 1348kJ; Protein 13g; Carbohydrate 12g, of which sugars 10g; Fat 25g, of which saturates 5g; Cholesterol 24mg; Calcium 147mg; Fibre 3.0g; Sodium 263mg.

Tomato and mozzarella toasts

These are made from sfilatini (thin ciabatta) and are ideal served with drinks before a meal. Prepare them several hours in advance and pop them in the oven just as your guests arrive.

SERVES 6–8

3 sfilatini (thin ciabatta)

about 250ml/8fl oz/1 cup sun-dried
   tomato paste

3 x 150g/5oz packets mozzarella
   cheese, drained

about 10ml/2 tsp dried oregano or
   mixed herbs

30–45ml/2–3 tbsp olive oil

ground black pepper

1 Cut each sfilatino on the diagonal into 12–15 slices, discarding the ends. Toast lightly on both sides.

2 Preheat the oven to 220°C/425°F/Gas 7. Spread sun-dried tomato paste on one side of each slice of toast. Cut the mozzarella into small pieces and arrange over the tomato paste.

3 Put the toasts on baking sheets, sprinkle with herbs and pepper to taste and drizzle with oil. Bake for 5 minutes or until the mozzarella has melted and is bubbling. Leave the toasts to settle for a few minutes before serving.

Nutritional information per portion: Energy 281kcal/1171kJ; Protein 14g; Carbohydrate 16g, of which sugars 5g; Fat 18g, of which saturates 9g; Cholesterol 33mg; Calcium 246mg; Fibre 3.3g; Sodium 418mg.

Toasted sfilatino with aromatic tomatoes

There are a great way to keep hunger pangs at bay while you wait for the main course. Simply grill the sliced sfilatino, heap on the sauce and drizzle over plenty of good extra virgin olive oil. To accompany, put out little bowls of pine nuts, lightly toasted in a pan.

SERVES 6

2 sfilatino (thin ciabatta), sliced lengthways
    into 3 pieces
1 garlic clove, cut in half
leaves from 4 fresh oregano sprigs
18 kalamata olives, stoned (pitted)
extra virgin olive oil, for drizzling
ground black pepper

FOR THE AROMATIC TOMATOES

800g/1³⁄₄lb ripe plum tomatoes
30ml/2 tbsp extra virgin olive oil
2 garlic cloves, crushed to a paste
    with a pinch of salt
1 small piece of dried chilli, seeds removed,
    finely chopped

1 For the aromatic tomatoes, plunge the tomatoes into boiling water for 30 seconds, then refresh in cold water. Peel away the skins, remove the seeds and core and roughly chop the flesh. Mix the oil and crushed garlic in a large frying pan.

2 Place the pan on the stove over high heat. Once the garlic starts to sizzle, add the tomatoes and the chilli; do not let the garlic burn. Cook for 2 minutes. (The aim is to evaporate the liquid rather than pulp the tomatoes, which should keep their shape.)

3 Under a hot grill (broiler), toast the bread on both sides, pressing down with a metal spatula to produce attractive stripes. Then, generously rub each slice with the cut side of a piece of garlic.

4 Roughly chop all but a few of the oregano leaves and mix them into the tomato sauce. Pile the mixture on to the toasted sfilatino. Sprinkle over the whole oregano leaves and the olive slivers. Add plenty of pepper, drizzle with lots of olive oil and serve immediately.

Nutritional information per portion: Energy 148kcal/ 620kJ; Protein 3g; Carbohydrate 14g, of which sugars 5g; Fat 9g, of which saturates 1g; Cholesterol 0mg; Calcium 38mg; Fibre 2.9g; Sodium 384mg.

Carpaccio of beef

The taste and texture of good raw fillet of beef is something to be savoured. The combination of ginger, garlic and soy sauce will add a tang to the final delicious melt-in-the-mouth experience.

SERVES 6–8

250ml/8fl oz/1 cup soy sauce

175ml/6fl oz/³⁄₄ cup vegetable oil

50ml/2fl oz/¹⁄₄ cup groundnut (peanut) oil

4 garlic cloves, crushed

2.5cm/1in fresh root ginger

450g/1lb fillet steak (beef tenderloin)

1 chunk Gruyère cheese

vinaigrette, to serve

1 Combine the soy sauce, vegetable oil, groundnut oil and garlic in a bowl. Peel and chop the ginger and add it to the bowl.

2 Marinate the fillet steak in the mixture for at least 4–5 hours or preferably overnight.

3 About 30–45 minutes before you are ready to serve, put the steak in the freezer to firm it up.

4 Slice the steak very thinly. Shave some of the cheese on top and drizzle with vinaigrette. Serve on a very cold plate.

Nutritional information per portion: Energy 447kcal/ 1853kJ; Protein 26g; Carbohydrate 3g, of which sugars 2g; Fat 37g, of which saturates 8g; Cholesterol 74mg; Calcium 58mg; Fibre 0g; Sodium 2308mg.

Italian prawn skewers

Parsley and lemon are all that is required to create a lovely tiger prawn dish. Grill them, or barbecue them, and serve with lemon wedges and watercress for an alfresco summer appetizer.

SERVES 4

900g/2lb raw tiger prawns
   (jumbo shrimp), peeled
60ml/4 tbsp olive oil
45ml/3 tbsp vegetable oil
75g/3oz/1¼ cups very fine
   dry breadcrumbs
1 garlic clove, crushed
15ml/1 tbsp chopped fresh parsley
salt and ground black pepper
lemon wedges, to serve
watercress, to serve

1 Slit the prawns down their backs and remove the dark vein. Rinse in cold water and dry on kitchen paper.

2 Mix the oils in a large bowl and add the prawns, coating them evenly. Add the breadcrumbs, garlic and parsley, and season. Toss the prawns thoroughly, to give them an even coating of breadcrumbs. Cover and leave to marinate for 1 hour.

3 Carefully thread the tiger prawns on to four metal or wooden skewers, curling them up as you work, so that the tails are skewered neatly in the middle.

4 Preheat the grill (broiler) to a moderate heat. Place the skewers in the grill (broiling) pan and cook for 2 minutes on each side, until they are golden. Serve with the lemon.

Nutritional information per portion: Energy 415kcal/1734kJ; Protein 42.2g; Carbohydrate 14.9g, of which sugars 0.8g; Fat 21.1g, of which saturates 2.8g; Cholesterol 439mg; Calcium 227mg; Fibre 1.1g; Sodium 574mg.

Genoese squid salad

This traditional salad is perfect for summer picnics, when green beans and new potatoes are at their best. It also makes a tasty light lunch and a delicious first course.

SERVES 4–6

450g/1lb prepared squid, cut into rings

4 garlic cloves, roughly chopped

300ml/½ pint/1¼ cups Italian
    red wine

450g/1lb waxy new potatoes,
    scrubbed clean

225g/8oz green beans, trimmed and
    cut into short lengths

2–3 drained sun-dried tomatoes in oil,
    thinly sliced lengthways

60ml/4 tbsp extra virgin olive oil

15ml/1 tbsp red wine vinegar

salt and ground black pepper

1 Preheat the oven to 180°C/350°F/ Gas 4. Put the squid rings in an ovenproof dish with half the garlic, the wine and pepper to taste. Cover and cook for 45 minutes or until the squid is tender.

2 Put the potatoes in a pan, cover with cold water and add a good pinch of salt. Bring to the boil, cover and simmer for 15–20 minutes or until tender. Using a slotted spoon, lift out the potatoes and set aside. Add the beans to the boiling water and cook for 3 minutes. Drain.

3 When the potatoes are cool, slice them thickly on the diagonal and place them in a bowl with the warm beans and sun-dried tomatoes. Whisk the oil, wine vinegar and the remaining garlic in a jug (pitcher) and add salt and pepper to taste. Pour over the potato mixture.

4 Drain the squid and discard the wine and garlic. Add the squid to the potato mixture and fold very gently to mix. Arrange the salad on individual plates and grind pepper liberally all over. Serve warm.

Nutritional information per portion: Energy 198kcal/ 2380kJ; Protein 13g; Carbohydrate 7g, of which sugars 1g; Fat 13g, of which saturates 2g; Cholesterol 169mg; Calcium 28mg; Fibre 1.5g; Sodium 234mg.

Tuna carpaccio

Fillet of beef is most often used for carpaccio, but meaty fish like tuna – and swordfish – make an unusual change. The secret is to slice the fish wafer thin, made possible by freezing the fish first.

SERVES 4

2 fresh tuna steaks, about 450g/1lb total weight
60ml/4 tbsp extra virgin olive oil
15ml/1 tbsp balsamic vinegar
5ml/1 tsp caster (superfine) sugar
30ml/2 tbsp drained bottled green peppercorns or capers
salt and ground black pepper
lemon wedges and green salad, to serve

1 Remove the skin from each tuna steak and place each steak between two sheets of clear film (plastic wrap) or baking parchment. Pound with a rolling pin until flattened slightly.

2 Roll up the tuna as tightly as possible, then wrap tightly in clear film and place in the freezer for 4 hours or until firm.

3 Unwrap the tuna and cut crossways into the thinnest possible slices. Arrange on individual plates.

4 Whisk together the remaining ingredients, season and pour over the tuna. Cover and allow to come to room temperature for 30 minutes before serving with lemon wedges and a green salad.

Nutritional information per portion:Energy 294kcal/ 1223kJ; Protein 27g; Carbohydrate 1g, of which sugars 1g; Fat 20g, of which saturates 3g; Cholesterol 32mg; Calcium 18mg; Fibre 0g; Sodium 151mg.

Gnocchi, polenta and pasta

Pasta is available in a wide variety of shapes, sizes and flavours, and creates the basis for many delicious dishes. Freshly cooked pasta, topped or tossed with a tasty sauce and served with crusty Italian bread, provides an appealing meal for all to enjoy. Polenta is a popular accompaniment that is usually served with the main course, especially with meaty casseroles.

Spinach and ricotta gnocchi

The mixture for these tasty little herb dumplings, known as gnocchi, needs to be handled very carefully to achieve light and fluffy results. Serve with a sage butter and grated Parmesan.

SERVES 6

6 garlic cloves, unpeeled
25g/1oz mixed fresh herbs, such as parsley,
    basil, thyme, coriander (cilantro) and chives,
    finely chopped
225g/8oz fresh spinach leaves
250g/9oz/generous 1 cup ricotta cheese

1 egg yolk
50g/2oz/^{2}/$_3$ cup grated Parmesan cheese
75g/3oz/^{2}/$_3$ cup plain (all-purpose) flour
50g/2oz/^{1}/$_4$ cup butter
30ml/2 tbsp fresh sage, chopped
salt and ground black pepper

1 Cook the garlic cloves in boiling water for 4 minutes. Drain and squeeze out of the skins. Place in a food processor or blender with the herbs and blend to a purée, or mash the garlic with a fork and add the herbs to mix well.

2 Place the spinach in a large pan with just the water that clings to the leaves, and cook gently until wilted. Leave to cool, then squeeze out as much liquid as possible. Chop finely.

3 Place the ricotta in a bowl and beat in the egg yolk, spinach, herbs and garlic. Stir in half the Parmesan, sift in the flour and mix well.

4 Using floured hands, break off pieces of the mixture slightly smaller than a walnut and roll into small dumplings.

5 Bring a large pan of salted water to the boil and carefully add the gnocchi. When they rise to the top of the pan they are cooked; this should take about 3 minutes.

6 The gnocchi should be light and fluffy all the way through. If not, simmer for a further minute. Drain well. Meanwhile, melt the butter in a frying pan and add the sage. Simmer gently for 1 minute. Add the gnocchi to the frying pan and toss in the butter over a gentle heat for about 1 minute, then serve, sprinkled with the remaining Parmesan.

Nutritional information per portion: Energy 193kcal/ 803kJ; Protein 7g; Carbohydrate 12g, of which sugars 2g; Fat 13g, of which saturates 8g; Cholesterol 72mg; Calcium 227mg; Fibre 2g; Sodium 213mg.

Gnocchi with gorgonzola sauce

All over Italy in the different regions, gnocchi are prepared using a variety of ingredients.
In this recipe, gnocchi di patate, potato dumplings, are served with a creamy cheese sauce.

SERVES 4

450g/1lb floury potatoes, unpeeled,
    cooked and drained
1 large egg
115g/4oz/1 cup plain (all-purpose) flour
fresh thyme sprigs, to garnish
salt and ground black pepper

FOR THE SAUCE
115g/4oz Gorgonzola cheese
60ml/4 tbsp double (heavy) cream
15ml/1 tbsp fresh thyme, chopped
60ml/4 tbsp freshly grated
    Parmesan cheese, to serve

1 Remove the skins from the potatoes. Force them through a sieve (strainer) into a bowl. Season, then beat in the egg until incorporated. Add the flour a little at a time, stirring until you have a smooth dough. (You may not need all the flour.) Knead for about 3 minutes on a floured surface, until it is smooth.

2 Divide the dough into 6 equal pieces and gently roll each piece into a log shape. Cut each log into 6–8 pieces, about 2.5cm/1in long, then gently roll each piece in the flour. Gently press each piece on to the floured surface with the tines of a fork to leave ridges in the dough.

3 To cook, drop the gnocchi into a pan of boiling water. Once they rise to the surface, cook for 4–5 minutes more. Remove and drain.

4 Place the Gorgonzola, cream and thyme in a pan and heat gently until the cheese melts to form a creamy consistency, and heat through. Add the drained gnocchi and combine. Serve with Parmesan and garnish with thyme.

Nutritional information per portion: Energy 430kcal/1801kJ; Protein 18.1g; Carbohydrate 40.9g, of which sugars 2.3g; Fat 23.6g, of which saturates 13.5g; Cholesterol 104mg; Calcium 386mg; Fibre 2g; Sodium 562mg.

Polenta elisa

This dish comes from the valley around Lake Como. Serve it solo as an appetizer, or with a mixed salad and some sliced salami or prosciutto for a midweek supper.

SERVES 4

250ml/8fl oz/1 cup milk
225g/8oz/2 cups pre-cooked polenta
115g/4oz/1 cup grated Gruyère cheese
115g/4oz/1 cup Dolcelatte
   cheese, crumbled
50g/2oz/¼ cup butter
2 garlic cloves, roughly chopped
a few fresh sage leaves, chopped
salt and ground black pepper
prosciutto, to serve

1 Preheat the oven to 200°C/400°F/Gas 6. Lightly butter a baking dish.

2 Bring the milk and 750ml/1¼ pints/3 cups water to the boil in a large pan, add 5ml/1 tsp salt, then pour in the polenta. Cook for about 8 minutes or according to the instructions on the packet.

3 Spoon half the polenta into the baking dish and level. Cover with half the grated Gruyère and crumbled Dolcelatte. Spoon the remaining polenta evenly over the top and sprinkle with the remaining cheeses.

4 Melt the butter in a small pan until foaming, add the garlic and sage and fry, stirring, until the butter turns golden brown. Drizzle the butter mixture over the polenta and cheese and grind black pepper liberally over the top. Bake for 5 minutes. Serve hot, with slices of prosciutto.

Nutritional information per portion: Energy 570kcal/ 2366kJ; Protein 22g; Carbohydrate 44g, of which sugars 3g; Fat 33g, of which saturates 20g; Cholesterol 514mg; Calcium 514mg; Fibre 2.5g; Sodium 552mg.

Grilled polenta with mushrooms

This is a quick and easy way to use up leftover polenta. You can vary the flavour by using fried onions instead of mushrooms if you prefer, or make it really Venetian by adding some warm, braised radicchio leaves. Asiago is a local cheese of the Veneto and is much prized in cooking.

SERVES 4

1.75 litres/3 pints/7½ cups boiling water

200–225g/7–8oz/scant 2 cups polenta flour

200g/7oz Gorgonzola cheese, sliced

45ml/3 tbsp olive oil

250g/9oz Asiago or Fontina cheese, cubed

a little milk

400g/14oz/5½ cups mushrooms, sliced

2 garlic cloves, thinly sliced

45ml/3 tbsp finely chopped fresh flat leaf
   parsley, to garnish

sea salt and ground black pepper

1 First, make the polenta: put the water into a wide, heavy pan over high heat and bring back to the boil. Add a large pinch of salt. Trickle the polenta flour into the boiling water in a fine rain with one hand, while whisking constantly with the other.

2 When all the polenta flour has been whisked into the water, reduce the heat to medium-low. Stir with a strong, long-handled wooden spoon until the polenta comes away from the sides of the pan. This will take 40–50 minutes.

3 Turn the polenta out on to a board and pat it into a square shape with a spatula. Leave it to rest for 5 minutes. Cut the polenta into eight squares.

4 Heat the grill (broiler) and lightly oil the polenta squares. Put the cheeses in a heatproof bowl and add milk to cover. Set it over a pan of simmering water and allow the cheeses to melt and blend with the milk, stirring frequently.

5 Meanwhile, put the remaining oil in a frying pan over medium heat and fry the mushrooms and garlic, stirring frequently, for 10 minutes, until the mushrooms are cooked. Season. When the cheese and milk have formed a smooth sauce, grill (broil) the polenta on both sides.

6 Arrange two squares of grilled polenta on each plate and cover with a spoonful of the melted cheese. Spoon the mushrooms evenly over the top, then sprinkle each portion with chopped flat leaf parsley and serve immediately.

Nutritional information per portion: Energy 518kcal/2155kJ; Protein 18.9g; Carbohydrate 46.2g, of which sugars 0.3g; Fat 27.2g, of which saturates 16.1g; Cholesterol 69mg; Calcium 334mg; Fibre 2.5g; Sodium 397mg.

Creamy polenta with Dolcelatte

Soft-cooked polenta is a great accompaniment to meat dishes and makes a delicious change from the usual potatoes or rice. It can also be enjoyed on its own as a hearty snack.

SERVES 4–6

900ml/1½ pints/3¾ cups milk
115g/4oz/1 cup instant polenta
60ml/4 tbsp extra virgin olive oil
115g/4oz Dolcelatte cheese
salt and ground black pepper

1 In a large pan, bring the milk to the boil, then add a good pinch of salt.

2 Remove the pan from the heat and pour in the polenta in a slow, steady stream, stirring constantly to combine.

3 Return the pan to a low heat, simmer gently, stirring constantly, for 5 minutes. Remove the pan from the heat and stir in the olive oil.

4 Spoon into a serving dish and sprinkle with the cheese. Season and serve.

Nutritional information per portion: Energy 271kcal/1131kJ; Protein 10.8g; Carbohydrate 21.1g, of which sugars 7.1g; Fat 16.1g, of which saturates 6.3g; Cholesterol 23mg; Calcium 274mg; Fibre 0.4g; Sodium 298mg.

Stuffed polenta fritters

These stuffed polenta fritters make a tasty treat. Anchovies are the traditional filling but here a little tomato, rosemary and cheese have been used. Porcini mushrooms make a good alternative.

SERVES 6

250g/9oz/1½ cups polenta
30–45ml/2–3 tbsp tomato paste
30–45ml/2–3 tbsp diced ripe fresh or
   canned chopped tomatoes
30ml/2 tbsp chopped fresh rosemary
30–45ml/2–3 tbsp freshly grated
   Parmesan or Pecorino cheese
130g/4½oz mozzarella, Gorgonzola or
   Fontina cheese, finely chopped
half vegetable and half olive oil,
   for frying
1–2 eggs, lightly beaten
plain (all-purpose) flour, for dusting
salt
diced red (bell) pepper, shredded lettuce
   and rosemary sprigs, to garnish

1 In a large pan, mix the polenta with 250ml/8fl oz/1 cup cold water and stir. Add 750ml/1¼ pints/3 cups boiling water, bring to the boil and cook, stirring, for 30 minutes until the mixture is thick. Season. Pour into an oiled baking dish to a depth of 1cm/½ inch. Chill.

2 Using a pastry (cookie) cutter, cut the polenta into rounds. Combine the tomato paste with the tomatoes. Spread a little of the mixture on the soft, moist side of a polenta round.

3 Sprinkle with rosemary and cheese, top with another round of polenta, and press the edges together. Fill the remaining polenta rounds in the same way.

4 Pour a 5cm/2in depth of oil into a large frying pan, and heat until hot enough to brown a cube of bread in 30 seconds. Dip a sandwich into the egg, then the flour. Fry for 4–5 minutes, turning once. Drain, and cook the remaining polenta. Garnish with pepper, lettuce and rosemary.

Nutritional information per portion: Energy 333kcal/1386kJ; Protein 11.4g; Carbohydrate 31.8g, of which sugars 1.3g; Fat 17.5g, of which saturates 5.3g; Cholesterol 49mg; Calcium 148mg; Fibre 1.2g; Sodium 171mg.

Grilled polenta with caramelized onions, radicchio and taleggio cheese

Slices of grilled polenta are one of the staples of north Italian cooking. Here they are topped with slowly caramelized onions and bubbling Taleggio cheese, also from north Italy.

SERVES 4

900ml/1¹/₂ pints/3³/₄ cups water
5ml/1 tsp salt
150g/5oz/generous 1 cup polenta
    or cornmeal
50g/2oz/¹/₃ cup freshly grated
    Parmesan cheese
5ml/1 tsp chopped fresh thyme
90ml/6 tbsp olive oil
675g/1¹/₂lb onions, halved and sliced

2 garlic cloves, chopped
a few fresh thyme sprigs
5ml/1 tsp brown sugar
15–30ml/1–2 tbsp balsamic vinegar
2 heads radicchio, cut into thick slices
    or wedges
225g/8oz Taleggio cheese, sliced
salt and ground black pepper

1 In a large pan, bring the water to the boil and add the salt. Adjust the heat so that it simmers. Stirring all the time, add the polenta in a steady stream, then bring to the boil. Cook over a very low heat, stirring frequently, for 30–40 minutes, until thick and smooth.

2 Beat in the Parmesan and chopped thyme, then turn on to a work surface or tray. Spread evenly to form a layer 1cm/¹/₂ inch thick, then leave to cool.

3 Heat 30ml/2 tbsp of the oil in a frying pan over a moderate heat. Add the onions and stir to coat in the oil, then cover and cook over a very low heat for 15 minutes, stirring occasionally.

4 Add the garlic and most of the thyme sprigs and cook, uncovered, for another 10 minutes, or until light brown.

5 Add the sugar, 15ml/1 tbsp of the vinegar and salt and pepper. Cook for another 5–10 minutes, until soft and well-browned. Taste and add more vinegar and seasoning as necessary.

6 Preheat the grill (broiler). Cut the polenta into thick slices and brush with a little of the remaining oil, then grill (broil) until the slices are crusty and lightly browned.

7 Turn over the polenta and add the radicchio to the grill rack or pan. Season the radicchio and brush with a little oil. Grill for about 5 minutes, until the polenta and radicchio are browned. Drizzle a little vinegar over the radicchio.

8 Heap the onions on to the polenta. Sprinkle the cheese and a few sprigs of thyme over both polenta and radicchio. Grill until the cheese is bubbling. Season with pepper and serve immediately.

Nutritional information per portion: Energy 617kcal/2563kJ; Protein 26.5g; Carbohydrate 43.9g, of which sugars 12.6g; Fat 36.6g, of which saturates 13.9g; Cholesterol 52mg; Calcium 676mg; Fibre 4.3g; Sodium 705mg.

Orecchiette with garlic and chilli

All pasta shapes work well in this incredibly fiery pasta dish, but orecchiette are particularly suitable, since their blandness and chewy texture act as a perfect foil for the hot sauce.

SERVES 4

150ml/¼ pint/⅔ cup olive oil
3 garlic cloves
4 whole dried red chillies
60ml/4 tbsp tomato paste
400g/14oz dried orecchiette

1 Bring a large pan of salted water to the boil.

2 Heat the oil in a different large pan. Add the garlic and chillies and fry over low to medium heat for 3–4 minutes, until the garlic is soft and golden brown, and the chillies are very shiny and swollen. Do not let either burn.

3 Scoop the garlic and chillies out of the oil with a slotted spoon. Put the garlic and chillies in a food processor or blender and add the tomato paste. Process until smooth, then stir back into the oil remaining in the pan.

4 Add the pasta to the boiling water. Cook for 12–14 minutes until just tender, then drain. Transfer it to the pan containing the garlic and chilli mixture. Toss over the heat until the pasta is coated with the sauce. Serve.

Nutritional information per portion: Energy 577kcal/2424kJ; Protein 12.7g; Carbohydrate 76g, of which sugars 5.2g; Fat 26.8g, of which saturates 3.7g; Cholesterol 0mg; Calcium 32mg; Fibre 3.3g; Sodium 39mg.

Stuffed pasta shells

This makes an excellent dinner party appetizer for six people. If you want to serve more people, there will be more than enough filling.

SERVES 6

18 large pasta shells for stuffing
25g/1oz/2 tbsp butter
1 small onion, finely chopped
275g/10oz fresh spinach leaves, trimmed, washed and shredded
1 garlic clove, crushed
1 sachet of saffron powder
nutmeg
250g/9oz/generous 1 cup ricotta cheese
1 egg
1 quantity Basic Tomato Sauce, see page 211
about 150ml/^{1}/$_4$ pint/^{2}/$_3$ cup dry white wine, vegetable stock or water
100ml/3^1/$_2$fl oz/scant ^{1}/$_2$ cup double (heavy) cream
50g/2oz/^{2}/$_3$ cup freshly grated Parmesan cheese
salt and ground black pepper

1 Preheat the oven to 190°C/375°F/Gas 5. In a large pan, cook the pasta shells for 10 minutes, until tender. Drain them and place in cold water.

2 Melt the butter in a pan, add the onion and cook gently until soft. Add the spinach, garlic and saffron, then grate in plenty of nutmeg and season. Cook for 5–8 minutes, stirring until the spinach is wilted and tender.

3 Increase the heat and stir until the water is driven off and the spinach is quite dry. Transfer the spinach to a bowl, add the ricotta and beat well to mix. Taste for seasoning, then add the egg and beat well again.

4 Combine the tomato sauce with the wine, stock or water. Add the cream, mix well and season. Spread half the sauce over six gratin dishes. Remove the pasta shells from the water, drain, and fill them with the spinach mixture. Divide the shells between the dishes, spoon over the remaining sauce, then cover with the grated Parmesan. Bake for 10–12 minutes.

Nutritional information per portion: Energy 358kcal/1505kJ; Protein 11.6g; Carbohydrate 43.3g, of which sugars 7.7g; Fat 16.7g, of which saturates 5.6g; Cholesterol 20mg; Calcium 56mg; Fibre 2.9g; Sodium 542mg.

Ravioli in the pesaro style

A recipe for ravioli with a ricotta cheese and spinach filling exists in most parts of Italy. Instead of spinach, Swiss chard can be used, or it could even be substituted by fresh young nettles.

SERVES 6

about 400g/14oz/3^{1}/$_{2}$ cups plain
   (all-purpose) flour
50g/2oz/2 tbsp fine semolina,
   plus extra for dusting
4 eggs
1 egg yolk
350g/12oz fresh ricotta cheese

500g/1^{1}/$_{4}$lb spinach, cooked and finely chopped
grated rind of 1 large unwaxed lemon
sea salt and ground black pepper
115g/4oz/1^{1}/$_{4}$ cups freshly grated
   mild Pecorino cheese, to serve
Basic Tomato Sauce, *see* page 211, or melted
   butter, to serve

1 Mix together the flour and semolina and place the mixture on a work surface in a mound. Use your fist to make a hollow in the centre.

2 Beat the eggs and egg yolk together and pour the mixture into the hollow in the flour. Work the flour and eggs together with your fingertips until you have a pliable ball of dough that is neither too sticky, or too dry – add more flour as required.

3 Knead the ball of dough until it is smooth and elastic. Cover with a clean cloth or wrap in clear film (plastic wrap), and leave to rest for about 30 minutes while you make the filling for the ravioli.

4 In a large bowl, mix together the ricotta cheese, chopped spinach and grated lemon rind. Season to taste with salt and pepper.

5 Roll out the pasta into a long, thin rectangle as finely and as evenly as possible. Drop the filling, in a neat row, along half the sheet of pasta, a scant tablespoon at a time, leaving about 2.5cm/1in between the little mounds of filling. Fold the sheet over to cover the filling.

6 With your fingers, press down firmly between the mounds of filling so that the pasta sticks together and closes up like a little parcel. Cut out the ravioli with a serrated pasta cutter or knife and press round the edges again to make sure each is perfectly sealed.

7 Dust a wide baking tray with semolina and lay the ravioli over it, taking care not to overlap them or lay them on top of one another.

8 Bring a large pan of water to the boil and drop in the ravioli. Cook for 3–4 minutes, in batches. They should rise to the surface when cooked. Scoop out the ravioli using a large slotted spoon as soon as they are cooked, and transfer them to a warmed bowl.

9 Dress the ravioli with tomato sauce or melted butter and sprinkle with freshly grated Pecorino cheese.

Nutritional information per portion: Energy 513kcal/2155kJ; Protein 26.3g; Carbohydrate 61.2g, of which sugars 3.8g; Fat 19.8g, of which saturates 10g; Cholesterol 201mg; Calcium 489mg; Fibre 4g; Sodium 377mg.

Mushroom and courgette lasagne

This is the perfect main-course lasagne for vegetarians. Adding dried porcini to fresh chestnut mushrooms intensifies the "mushroomy" flavour and gives the whole dish more substance.

SERVES 6

15g/¹/₂oz dried porcini mushrooms
175ml/6fl oz/³/₄ cup warm water
30ml/2 tbsp olive oil
75g/3oz/6 tbsp butter
450g/1lb courgettes (zucchini), thinly sliced
1 onion, finely chopped
450g/1lb/6 cups brown cap (cremini)
    mushrooms, sliced
2 garlic cloves, crushed
1 quantity Basic Tomato Sauce, *see page 211*
10ml/2 tsp chopped fresh marjoram
    or 5ml/1 tsp dried marjoram, plus

extra fresh leaves, to garnish
6–8 "no pre-cook" lasagne sheets
50g/2oz/²/₃ cup freshly grated Parmesan cheese
salt and ground black pepper

FOR THE WHITE SAUCE
40g/1¹/₂oz/3 tbsp butter
40g/1¹/₂oz/1/3 cup plain (all-purpose) flour
900ml/1¹/₂ pints/3³/₄ cups hot milk
nutmeg

1 Put the dried porcini mushrooms in a bowl. Pour over the warm water and leave to soak for 15–20 minutes. Transfer the porcini and liquid to a fine sieve (strainer) set over a bowl, and squeeze them with your hands to release as much liquid as possible. Chop the mushrooms finely and set aside. Strain the soaking liquid through a fine sieve and reserve half for the sauce.

2 Preheat the oven to 190°C/375°F/Gas 5. Heat the olive oil with 25g/1oz/2 tbsp of the butter in a large skillet or pan. Add about half the courgette slices to the pan and season with salt and pepper to taste. Cook them over medium heat, turning the slices frequently, for 5–8 minutes until they are lightly coloured on both sides.

3 Remove the courgettes from the pan with a slotted spoon and allow to drain on kitchen paper. Repeat with the remaining courgettes.

4 Melt half the remaining butter in the fat remaining in the pan, then cook the finely chopped onion, stirring, for 1–2 minutes. Add half of the fresh mushrooms and the crushed garlic to the pan and sprinkle with a little salt and pepper to taste.

5 Toss the mushrooms over high heat for 5 minutes or so until the mushrooms are juicy and tender. Transfer to a bowl with a slotted spoon, then repeat with the remaining butter and mushrooms.

6 Make the white sauce. Melt the butter in a large pan, add the flour and cook, stirring, over medium heat for 1–2 minutes. Add the hot milk a little at a time, whisking well after each addition. Bring to the boil and cook, stirring, until the sauce is smooth and thick. Grate in fresh nutmeg to taste and season with a little salt and pepper. Whisk well, then remove the sauce from the heat.

7 Place the tomato sauce in a blender or food processor with the reserved porcini liquid and blend to a pureé. Add the courgettes to the bowl of fried mushrooms and stir in the porcini and marjoram. Season, then spread a third of the tomato sauce in a baking dish. Add half the vegetable mixture.

8 Top with a third of the white sauce, then half the lasagne sheets. Repeat these layers, then top with the remaining tomato sauce and white sauce and sprinkle with the grated Parmesan cheese.

9 Bake the lasagne for 35–40 minutes, or until the pasta feels tender when pierced with a skewer. Stand for about 10 minutes before serving. If you like, sprinkle each serving with marjoram leaves.

Nutritional information per portion: Energy 421kcal/1757kJ; Protein 15.5g; Carbohydrate 32.9g, of which sugars 15g; Fat 26.2g, of which saturates 12.4g; Cholesterol 49mg; Calcium 346mg; Fibre 3.8g; Sodium 310mg.

Sardinian ravioli

These ravioli from northern Sardinia are known as 'culurgiones'. They are gratinéed in the oven with butter and cheese, but are also often served with a tomato sauce.

SERVES 4–6

1 quantity Pasta with Eggs, *see page 195*
50g/2oz/¼ cup butter
50g/2oz/⅔ cup freshly grated Pecorino cheese

FOR THE FILLING
2 potatoes, each about 200g/7oz, diced
65g/2½oz/generous ⅔ cup freshly grated hard
   salted Pecorino cheese

75g/3oz soft fresh Pecorino cheese
1 egg yolk
1 large bunch fresh mint, leaves removed
   and chopped
good pinch of saffron powder
salt and ground black pepper

1 Make the filling. Cook the potatoes in salted boiling water for 15–20 minutes, until soft. Drain and transfer to a bowl, then mash until smooth. Leave until cold. Add the cheeses, egg yolk, mint and saffron, season to taste and stir well to mix.

2 Using a pasta machine, roll out one-quarter of the pasta into a 90cm–1 metre/36in–3 foot strip. Cut the strip with a sharp knife into two 45–50cm/18–20in lengths.

3 With a fluted 10cm/4in pastry (cookie) cutter, cut out 4–5 discs from one of the pasta strips. Using a heaped teaspoon, put a mound of filling on one side of each disc. Brush a little water around the edge, then fold the plain side of the disc over the filling to make a half-moon shape. Pleat the curved edge to seal the discs and form crescents.

4 Put the crescents on floured dish towels, sprinkle with flour and leave to dry. Repeat with the remaining dough to make 32–40 crescents altogether.

5 Preheat the oven to 190°C/375°F/Gas 5. Cook the crescents in a large pan of salted boiling water for about 4–5 minutes. Meanwhile, melt the butter in a small pan.

6 Drain the crescents, transfer to a large baking dish and pour the melted butter over them. Sprinkle with the grated Pecorino and bake for 10–15 minutes until golden and bubbly. Allow to stand for 5 minutes before serving.

Nutritional information per portion: Energy 393kcal/1655kJ; Protein 16.1g; Carbohydrate 50.9g, of which sugars 2.8g; Fat 15.3g, of which saturates 8.7g; Cholesterol 71mg; Calcium 269mg; Fibre 2.6g; Sodium 271mg.

Macaroni with four cheeses

Rich and creamy, this is a deluxe macaroni cheese that can be served for an informal lunch or supper party. It goes well with a tomato and basil salad or a leafy green salad.

SERVES 4

250g/9oz/2¹/₄ cups short-cut macaroni
50g/2oz/¹/₄ cup butter
50g/2oz/¹/₂ cup plain (all-purpose) flour
600ml/1 pint/2¹/₂ cups milk
100ml/3¹/₂ fl oz/scant ¹/₂ cup double (heavy) cream
100ml/3¹/₂ fl oz/scant ¹/₂ cup dry white wine
50g/2oz/¹/₂ cup grated Gruyère or Emmental cheese
50g/2oz Fontina cheese, diced small
50g/2oz Gorgonzola cheese, crumbled
75g/3oz/1 cup freshly grated Parmesan cheese
salt and ground black pepper

1 Preheat the oven to 180°C/350°F/ Gas 4. Cook the pasta according to the instructions on the packet.

2 Meanwhile, gently melt the butter in a pan, add the flour and cook, stirring, for 1–2 minutes. Add the milk a little at a time, whisking after each addition. Stir in the cream, followed by the dry white wine. Bring to the boil. Cook, stirring until the sauce thickens, then remove the sauce from the heat.

3 Add the Gruyère or Emmental, Fontina, Gorgonzola and about a third of the grated Parmesan to the sauce. Stir well to mix in the cheeses, then taste for seasoning and add salt and pepper if needed.

4 Drain the pasta well and transfer to a baking dish. Pour the sauce over the pasta and mix, then sprinkle the remaining Parmesan over the top. Bake for 25–30 minutes or until golden brown. Serve hot.

Nutritional information per portion: Energy 523kcal/2202kJ; Protein 20.6g; Carbohydrate 69.7g, of which sugars 6.6g; Fat 19.3g, of which saturates 11.7g; Cholesterol 51mg; Calcium 349mg; Fibre 2.5g; Sodium 349mg.

Conchiglie with chicken livers and herbs

Fresh herbs and chicken livers are a classic combination, often used together on crostini in Tuscany. Here they are tossed with pasta shells to make a very tasty supper dish.

SERVES 4

50g/2oz/¼ cup butter

115g/4oz pancetta or rindless streaky (fatty) bacon, diced

250g/9oz frozen chicken livers, thawed, drained and diced

2 garlic cloves, crushed

10ml/2 tsp chopped fresh sage

300g/11oz/2¾ cups dried conchiglie

150ml/¼ pint/⅔ cup dry white wine

4 ripe Italian plum tomatoes, peeled and diced

15ml/1 tbsp chopped fresh flat leaf parsley

salt and ground black pepper

1 Melt half the butter in a medium skillet or pan, add the pancetta or bacon and fry over medium heat until it is lightly coloured but not crisp.

2 Add the chicken livers, garlic, half the sage and plenty of pepper. Increase the heat and toss the livers for about 5 minutes, until they change colour all over. Cook the pasta according to the instructions on the packet.

3 Pour the wine over the chicken livers in the pan and let it sizzle, then lower the heat and simmer gently for 5 minutes. Add the remaining butter to the pan. As soon as it has melted, add the diced tomatoes, toss to mix, then add the remaining sage and the parsley. Stir well. Taste and add salt if needed.

4 Drain the pasta and transfer it to a warmed bowl. Pour the sauce over and toss well. Serve immediately.

Nutritional information per portion: Energy 528kcal/2220kJ; Protein 25.4g; Carbohydrate 59g, of which sugars 5.9g; Fat 20.2g, of which saturates 9.6g; Cholesterol 283mg; Calcium 38mg; Fibre 3.2g; Sodium 498mg.

Spaghetti with eggs, bacon and cream

An all-time favourite that needs no introduction. This version has plenty of pancetta or bacon and is not too creamy, but you can vary the amounts as you please.

SERVES 4

30ml/2 tbsp olive oil

1 small onion, finely chopped

8 pancetta or rindless smoked streaky (fatty) bacon rashers, cut into 1cm/¹/₂in strips

350g/12oz fresh or dried spaghetti

4 eggs

60ml/4 tbsp crème fraîche

60ml/4 tbsp freshly grated Parmesan cheese, plus extra to serve

salt and ground black pepper

1 Heat the oil in a large pan, add the chopped onion and cook over low heat, stirring frequently, for about 5 minutes until softened but not coloured.

2 Add the strips of pancetta or bacon to the onion in the pan and cook for about 10 minutes, stirring. Meanwhile, cook the pasta in a pan of salted boiling water according to the instructions on the packet until *al dente*.

3 Put the eggs, crème fraîche and grated Parmesan in a bowl. Grind in plenty of pepper, then beat everything together well.

4 Drain the pasta, pour it into the pan with the pancetta or bacon and toss well to mix. Turn the heat off under the pan. Immediately add the egg mixture and toss vigorously so that it cooks lightly and coats the pasta.

5 Divide among four warmed bowls and sprinkle with black pepper. Serve immediately, with extra grated Parmesan handed separately.

Nutritional information per portion: Energy 708kcal/2966kJ; Protein 30.7g; Carbohydrate 66.6g, of which sugars 4.2g; Fat 37.5g, of which saturates 15.5g; Cholesterol 261mg; Calcium 250mg; Fibre 2.8g; Sodium 824mg.

Spaghetti with meatballs

Meatballs simmered in a sweet and spicy tomato sauce are truly delicious with spaghetti. Children love them and you can easily leave out the chillies, if you wish.

SERVES 6–8

350g/12oz minced (ground) beef
1 egg
60ml/4 tbsp roughly chopped fresh
    flat leaf parsley
2.5ml/¹⁄₂ tsp crushed dried red chillies
1 thick slice white bread, crusts
    removed
30ml/2 tbsp milk
about 30ml/2 tbsp olive oil
300ml/¹⁄₂ pint/1¹⁄₄ cups passata
400ml/14fl oz/1³⁄₄ cups vegetable
    stock
5ml/1 tsp granulated (white) sugar
350–450g/12oz–1lb fresh spaghetti
salt and ground black pepper
freshly grated Parmesan cheese,
    to serve

1 Put the minced beef in a large bowl. Add the egg, half the parsley and half the crushed chillies. Season with plenty of salt and pepper.

2 Tear the bread into pieces and place in a bowl. Moisten with the milk. Leave to soak for a few minutes, then squeeze out the excess milk and crumble the bread over the meat mixture. Mix together with a spoon, then knead.

3 Wash your hands, rinse them under the cold tap, then pick up small pieces of the mixture and roll them between your palms to make about 40–60 balls. Place the meatballs on a tray and chill in the refrigerator for 30 minutes.

4 Heat the oil in a frying pan. Cook the meatballs in batches until browned on all sides. Pour the passata and stock into a large pan. Heat gently, then add the remaining chillies and the sugar, and season. Add the meatballs to the passata mixture, then bring to the boil. Lower the heat, cover and simmer for 20 minutes. Pour the sauce over the fresh pasta and toss gently. Sprinkle with the remaining parsley and serve with grated Parmesan handed separately.

Nutritional information per portion: Energy 324kcal/1364kJ; Protein 17.1g; Carbohydrate 40.3g, of which sugars 7.7g; Fat 11.6g, of which saturates 3.8g; Cholesterol 50mg; Calcium 51mg; Fibre 2.7g; Sodium 156mg.

Cheese cappellacci with bolognese sauce

In Emilia-Romagna it is traditional to serve these cappellacci *with a rich meat sauce, but if you prefer you can serve them with a tomato sauce, or just melted butter.*

SERVES 6

1 quantity Pasta with Eggs, see page 195
2 litres/3¹/₂ pints/8 cups beef stock
   made with stock cubes, or diluted
   canned consommé
freshly grated Parmesan cheese, to serve
basil leaves, to garnish

FOR THE FILLING
250g/9oz/generous 1 cup ricotta cheese
90g/3¹/₂oz Taleggio cheese, rind removed,
   diced very small
60ml/4 tbsp freshly grated Parmesan cheese
1 small egg
nutmeg
salt and ground black pepper

FOR THE BOLOGNESE MEAT SAUCE
25g/1oz/2 tbsp butter
15ml/1 tbsp olive oil
1 onion
2 carrots
2 celery sticks
2 garlic cloves
130g/4¹/₂oz pancetta or rindless streaky
   (fatty) bacon, diced
250g/9oz lean minced (ground) beef
250g/9oz lean minced (ground) pork
120ml/4fl oz/¹/₂ cup dry white wine
2 x 400g/14oz cans crushed Italian plum tomatoes
475–750ml/16fl oz–1¹/₄ pints/2–3 cups beef stock
100ml/3¹/₂fl oz/scant ¹/₂ cup double (heavy) cream

1 Make the filling. Put the ricotta, Taleggio and grated Parmesan in a bowl and mash together with a fork. Add the egg and freshly grated nutmeg and salt and pepper to taste and stir well to mix.

2 Using a pasta machine, roll out one-quarter of the pasta into a 90cm/36in strip. Cut the strip with a sharp knife into two 45cm/18in lengths.

3 Using a 6cm/2¹/₂in square ravioli cutter, cut 6–7 squares from one of the pasta strips. Using a teaspoon, put a mound of filling in the centre of each square. Brush a little water around the edge of each square, then fold the square diagonally in half. Press to seal.

4 Wrap the triangle around one of your index fingers, bringing the bottom two corners together. Pinch the ends together to seal, then press with your fingertip around the top edge of the filling to make an indentation so that the "hat" looks like a bishop's mitre.

5 Place the cappellacci on floured dish towels, sprinkle them lightly with flour and leave to dry while repeating the process with the remaining dough to make 48–56 cappellacci altogether.

6 Make the meat sauce. Heat the butter and oil in a pan until sizzling. Add the vegetables, garlic, and the pancetta or bacon and cook over medium heat, stirring, for 10 minutes or until softened.

7 Add the minced beef and pork, lower the heat and cook gently for 10 minutes, stirring frequently and breaking up any lumps in the meat with a wooden spoon. Stir in salt and pepper to taste, then add the wine and stir again. Simmer for about 5 minutes, or until reduced.

8 Add the tomatoes and 250ml/8fl oz/1 cup of the stock and bring to the boil. Stir well, then lower the heat, half-cover the pan with a lid and leave to simmer very gently for 2 hours. Stir occasionally and add more stock as it becomes absorbed. Add the double cream to the meat sauce. Stir well to mix, then simmer the sauce, without a lid, for another 30 minutes, stirring frequently.

9 Bring the stock to the boil in a large pan. Drop the cappellacci into the stock, bring back to the boil and boil for 4–5 minutes; drain the cappellacci and divide them among six warmed serving bowls. Spoon the hot bolognese sauce over the cappellacci and sprinkle with grated Parmesan and basil leaves. Serve immediately.

Nutritional information per portion: Energy 513kcal/2155kJ; Protein 26.3g; Carbohydrate 61.2g, of which sugars 3.8g; Fat 19.8g, of which saturates 10g; Cholesterol 201mg; Calcium 489mg; Fibre 4g; Sodium 377mg.

Ravioli with pork and turkey

This Roman-style ravioli, stuffed with minced meat and cheese, is scented with fresh sage and rosemary. It makes an attractive and substantial meal.

SERVES 4

1 quantity Pasta with Eggs, see page 195
50g/2oz/¼ cup butter
a large bunch of fresh sage, leaves removed
    and roughly chopped
60ml/4 tbsp freshly grated Parmesan cheese
extra sage leaves and freshly grated
    Parmesan cheese, to serve

FOR THE FILLING
25g/1oz/2 tbsp butter
150g/5oz minced (ground) pork

115g/4oz minced (ground) turkey
4 fresh sage leaves, finely chopped
1 sprig of fresh rosemary, leaves removed
    and finely chopped
30ml/2 tbsp dry white wine
65g/2½oz/generous ¼ cup ricotta cheese
45ml/3 tbsp freshly grated Parmesan cheese
1 egg
nutmeg
salt and ground black pepper

1 Make the filling. Melt the butter in a pan, add the minced pork and turkey and the herbs and cook gently for 5–6 minutes, stirring frequently and breaking up any lumps in the meat with a wooden spoon. Add salt and pepper to taste and stir well to mix thoroughly.

2 Add the wine to the pan and stir again. Simmer for 1–2 minutes until reduced slightly, then cover the pan and simmer gently for about 20 minutes, stirring occasionally. With a slotted spoon, transfer the meat to a bowl and leave to cool.

3 Add the ricotta and Parmesan cheeses to the bowl with the egg and freshly grated nutmeg to taste. Stir well to mix the ingredients thoroughly.

4 Using a pasta machine, roll out one-quarter of the pasta into a 90cm/35in strip. Cut the strip with a sharp knife into two 45cm/18in lengths (you can do this during rolling if the strip gets too long to manage).

5 Using a teaspoon, put 10–12 little mounds of the filling along one side of one of the pasta strips, spacing them evenly. Brush a little water on to the pasta strip around each mound, then fold the plain side of the pasta strip over the filling.

6 Starting from the folded edge, press down gently with your fingertips around each mound of filling, pushing the air out at the unfolded edge. Sprinkle lightly with flour. With a fluted pasta wheel, cut along each long side, then between each mound to make small square shapes. Dust lightly with flour.

7 Put the ravioli in a single layer on floured dish towels and leave to dry while repeating the process with the remaining pasta to make 80–96 ravioli altogether.

8 Drop the ravioli into a large pan of salted boiling water, and boil for 4–5 minutes.

9 While the ravioli are cooking, melt the butter in a small pan, add the fresh sage leaves and stir over medium to high heat until the sage leaves are sizzling in the butter.

10 Drain the ravioli and pour half into a warmed large bowl. Sprinkle with half the grated Parmesan, then half the sage butter. Repeat with the remaining ravioli, Parmesan and sage butter. Serve immediately, garnished with fresh sage leaves and extra grated Parmesan.

Nutritional information per portion: Energy 393kcal/1653kJ; Protein 20g; Carbohydrate 42g, of which sugars 2.2g; Fat 17.1g, of which saturates 9.4g; Cholesterol 85mg; Calcium 180mg; Fibre 1.6g; Sodium 236mg.

Cannelloni sorrentina-style

There's more than one way of making cannelloni. For this fresh-tasting dish, sheets of cooked lasagne are rolled around a tomato filling to make a delicious main course.

SERVES 4–6

60ml/4 tbsp olive oil

1 small onion, finely chopped

900g/2lb ripe Italian plum tomatoes, peeled
   and finely chopped

2 garlic cloves, crushed

1 large handful fresh basil leaves, shredded,
   plus extra basil leaves, to garnish

250ml/8fl oz/1 cup vegetable stock

250ml/8fl oz/1 cup dry white wine

30ml/2 tbsp sun-dried tomato paste

2.5ml/$\frac{1}{2}$ tsp sugar

16–18 fresh or dried lasagne sheets

250g/9oz/generous 1 cup ricotta cheese

130g/4$\frac{1}{2}$oz packet mozzarella cheese,
   drained and diced small

8 bottled anchovy fillets in olive oil, drained
   and halved lengthways

50g/2oz/$\frac{2}{3}$ cup freshly grated
   Parmesan cheese

salt and ground black pepper

1 Heat the oil in a medium pan, add the onion and cook gently, stirring frequently, for about 5 minutes until softened. Stir in the tomatoes, garlic and half the basil. Season with salt and pepper to taste and toss over medium to high heat for 5 minutes.

2 Scoop about half the tomato mixture out of the pan, place in a bowl and set it aside to cool.

3 Stir the vegetable stock, white wine, tomato paste and sugar into the tomato mixture remaining in the pan and simmer for about 20 minutes, stirring occasionally.

4 Meanwhile, cook the lasagne sheets in batches in a pan of salted boiling water, according to the instructions on the packet. Drain and separate the sheets of lasagne and lay them out flat on a clean dish towel.

5 Preheat the oven to 190°C/ 375°F/Gas 5. Add the ricotta and mozzarella to the tomato mixture in the bowl. Stir in the remaining basil and season to taste with salt and pepper.

6 Spread a little of the mixture over each lasagne sheet. Place an anchovy fillet across the width of each sheet, close to one of the short ends. Starting from the end with the anchovy, roll each lasagne sheet up like a Swiss roll (jelly roll).

7 Purée the tomato sauce in a blender or food processor. Spread a little of the tomato sauce over the bottom of a large baking dish. Arrange the cannelloni seam-side down in a single layer in the dish and spoon the remaining sauce over them.

8 Sprinkle the Parmesan over the top and bake for 20 minutes or until the topping is golden brown and bubbling. Serve hot, garnished with basil leaves.

Nutritional information per portion: Energy 476kcal/1995kJ; Protein 19.9g; Carbohydrate 45g, of which sugars 9.3g; Fat 22.4g, of which saturates 9.8g; Cholesterol 41mg; Calcium 238mg; Fibre 3.7g; Sodium 365mg.

Sicilian lasagne

Lasagne is not as traditional in Sicily as it is in northern Italy, but the Sicilians have their own version which is fairly simple to make, and just as tasty.

SERVES 6

1 small onion, finely chopped
1/2 carrot, finely chopped
1/2 celery stick, finely chopped
45ml/3 tbsp olive oil
250g/9oz boneless pork, diced
60ml/4 tbsp dry white wine
400g/14oz can chopped Italian
    plum tomatoes or 400ml/14fl oz/
      1²/₃ cups passata

200ml/7fl oz/scant 1 cup chicken stock
15ml/1 tbsp tomato paste
2 bay leaves
15ml/1 tbsp chopped fresh flat leaf parsley
250g/9oz fresh lasagne sheets, pre-cooked if necessary
2 hard-boiled eggs, sliced
125g/4¹/₂oz packet mozzarella cheese, drained and sliced
60ml/4 tbsp freshly grated Pecorino cheese
salt and ground black pepper

1 Heat 30ml/2 tbsp of the oil in a large pan, add the chopped vegetables and cook over medium heat, stirring frequently, for about 10 minutes.

2 Add the pork and fry for about 5 minutes, stirring occasionally, until well browned on all sides. Pour in the wine and let it bubble and reduce for a few minutes, then add the tomatoes or passata, the stock and the tomato paste.

3 Make a tear in each bay leaf to release the flavour, then add to the pan with the parsley and salt and pepper to taste, mixing well. Cover and cook for 30–40 minutes until the pork is tender, stirring from time to time. Take the pan off the heat and remove and discard the bay leaves from the sauce. Then, using a slotted spoon, lift the pieces of meat out of the sauce. Chop them roughly, then return them to the sauce. Stir well.

4 Preheat the oven to 190°C/375°F/Gas 5. Bring a pan of salted water to the boil. Cut the lasagne sheets into 2.5cm/1in strips and add them to the boiling water. Cook for 3–4 minutes until just al dente. Drain well, then stir the strips into the sauce.

5 Spread half the pasta and sauce mixture in a baking dish and cover with half the mozzarella and egg slices and half the grated Pecorino. Repeat the layers, then drizzle the remaining oil over the top. Bake for 30–35 minutes until golden and bubbling. Stand for about 10 minutes before serving.

Nutritional information per portion: Energy 308kcal/1297kJ; Protein 21g; Carbohydrate 37g, of which sugars 6.7g; Fat 8.8g, of which saturates 4.1g; Cholesterol 102mg; Calcium 116mg; Fibre 2.7g; Sodium 153mg.

Farfalle with smoked salmon and dill

This quick, luxurious sauce for pasta has become very fashionable in Italy. Dill is the classic herb for cooking with fish, but if you don't like its flavour, substitute parsley or a little fresh tarragon.

SERVES 4

6 spring onions (scallions), sliced

50g/2oz/¼ cup butter

90ml/6 tbsp dry white wine
or vermouth

450ml/¾ pint/scant 2 cups double
(heavy) cream

freshly grated nutmeg

225g/8oz smoked salmon

30ml/2 tbsp chopped fresh dill

freshly squeezed lemon juice

450g/1lb/4 cups farfalle

salt and ground black pepper

fresh dill sprigs, to garnish

1 Using a sharp knife, slice the spring onions finely. Melt the butter in a large pan and fry the spring onions for about 1 minute, stirring occasionally, until softened.

2 Add the wine or vermouth and boil hard to reduce to about 30ml/2 tbsp. Stir in the cream and add salt, pepper and nutmeg to taste. Bring to the boil, then reduced to a simmer for 2–3 minutes until slightly thickened.

3 Cut the smoked salmon slices into 2.5cm/1in squares and stir into the sauce, together with the chopped fresh dill. Add a little lemon juice to taste. Keep warm while you cook the pasta.

4 Cook the pasta in a large pan of boiling salted water, following the instructions on the packet. Drain well. Toss with the sauce. Spoon into bowls and serve immediately, garnished with sprigs of dill.

Nutritional information per portion: Energy 624kcal/ 2632kJ; Protein 28g; Carbohydrate 86g, of which sugars 3g; Fat 21g, of which saturates 11g; Cholesterol 62mg; Calcium 55mg; Fibre 5.6g; Sodium 1248mg.

Spaghetti with salmon and prawns

This is a lovely fresh-tasting pasta dish, perfect for an alfresco meal in summer. Serve it as a main course lunch with warm ciabatta or focaccia and a dry white wine.

SERVES 4

300g/11oz salmon fillet

200ml/7fl oz/scant 1 cup dry white wine

a few fresh basil sprigs, plus extra basil leaves, to garnish

6 ripe Italian plum tomatoes, peeled and finely chopped

150ml/¼ pint/⅔ cup double (heavy) cream

350g/12oz/3 cups fresh or dried spaghetti

115g/4oz/⅔ cup peeled cooked prawns (shrimp), thawed and thoroughly dried if frozen

salt and ground black pepper

1 Put the salmon skin-side up in a pan. Pour the wine over, then add the basil sprigs and season. Bring the wine to the boil, cover and simmer gently for 5 minutes. Using a fish slice, lift the fish out of the pan and set aside to cool a little.

2 Add the cream and tomatoes to the liquid remaining in the pan and bring to the boil. Stir well, then lower the heat and simmer, uncovered, for 10–15 minutes.

3 Meanwhile, cook the pasta according to the packet instructions.

4 Flake the fish into large chunks, discarding the skin and any bones. Add the fish to the sauce with the prawns, shaking the pan until well coated. Taste for seasoning.

5 Drain the pasta and transfer to a warmed bowl. Pour the sauce over and toss to combine. Serve, garnished with fresh basil leaves.

Nutritional information per portion: Energy 701kcal/2941kJ; Protein 32.4g; Carbohydrate 70.4g, of which sugars 8.5g; Fat 30.6g, of which saturates 14.3g; Cholesterol 145mg; Calcium 94mg; Fibre 4.1g; Sodium 115mg.

Ravioli with crab

This modern recipe for a dinner party starter uses chilli-flavoured pasta, which looks and tastes good with the creamy filling of mascarpone cheese and crab.

SERVES 6

1 quantity chilli-flavoured Pasta with Eggs, *see* page 195
90g/3½oz/ 6 tbsp butter
juice of 1 lemon

FOR THE FILLING
175g/6oz/³/₄ cup mascarpone cheese
175g/6oz/³/₄ cup crabmeat

30ml/2 tbsp finely chopped fresh flat leaf parsley
finely grated rind of 1 lemon
pinch of crushed dried chillies (optional)
salt and ground black pepper

1 Make the filling. Put the mascarpone in a bowl and mash it with a fork. Add the crabmeat, parsley, lemon rind, crushed dried chillies (if using) and salt and pepper to taste. Stir well.

2 Using a pasta machine, roll out one-quarter of the pasta dough into a 90cm–1 metre/36in–3 foot strip. Cut the strip into two 45–50cm/18–20in lengths (you can do this during rolling if the strip is too long).

3 With a 6cm/2½in fluted pastry (cookie) cutter, cut out 8 squares from each pasta strip.

4 Using a teaspoon, put a mound of filling in the centre of half the discs. Brush a little water around the edge of the filled discs, then top with the plain discs and press the edges to seal. For a decorative finish, press the edges with the tines of a fork.

5 Put the ravioli on floured dish towels, sprinkle lightly with flour and leave to dry while repeating the process with the remaining dough to make 32 ravioli altogether.

6 Cook the ravioli in a large pan of salted boiling water for 4–5 minutes. Meanwhile, melt the butter and lemon juice in a small pan until sizzling. Drain the ravioli and divide them equally among four warmed bowls. Drizzle the lemon butter over the ravioli and serve immediately.

Nutritional information per portion: Energy 581kcal/2437kJ; Protein 22.6g; Carbohydrate 66.3g, of which sugars 4.4g; Fat 26.8g, of which saturates 15.9g; Cholesterol 98mg; Calcium 79mg; Fibre 2.6g; Sodium 380mg.

Vermicelli with squid ink

This recipe calls for strattu, a tasty sun-dried tomato paste, which is popular in Sicily. Good-quality concentrated tomato paste is the best substitute.

SERVES 4–6

whole fresh squid with ink sac
    (around 500g/1¼lb), washed,
    cleaned and prepared
60ml/4 tbsp olive oil
2–3 whole garlic cloves, bruised
45ml/3 tbsp chopped fresh parsley
100ml/3½fl oz/scant ½ cup
    dry white wine
15ml/1 tbsp strattu or 45ml/3 tbsp
    concentrated tomato paste
400g/14oz vermicelli
sea salt and ground black pepper

1 Cut the body of the squid into small cubes. Chop the tentacles finely. Rinse and dry the squid well.

2 Heat the olive oil over medium heat in a large pan. Add the garlic cloves, fry until brown, then remove with a slotted spoon and discard.

3 Add the squid to the garlic-flavoured oil. Stir in the parsley and plenty of pepper. Cover and simmer the mixture for 45 minutes.

4 Pour over the white wine and add the strattu or tomato paste. Stir well and simmer, uncovered, for 20 minutes.

5 Lower the heat, cover the pan again and cook for a further 30 minutes, adding a little hot water when needed to dilute the sauce.

6 About 15–17 minutes before serving, bring a pan of salted water to the boil. Add the pasta and cook for 10–12 minutes over medium heat until just tender. Meanwhile, add the ink sacs to the sauce and stir to mix.

7 Drain the pasta well and return it to the pan. Pour the sauce over and mix. Cover and leave to stand for 5 minutes, then serve immediately.

Nutritional information per portion: Energy 383kcal/1603kJ; Protein 18.9g; Carbohydrate 53.5g, of which sugars 0.3g; Fat 9.1g, of which saturates 1.4g; Cholesterol 188mg; Calcium 40mg; Fibre 0.3g; Sodium 100mg.

Pasta with mussels

The recipe is a famous speciality of Campo Marino, in the province of Salento in Puglia. Mussels are popular in the area, and the locals like to eat them raw with just a squeeze of lemon juice.

SERVES 4

500g/1¹/₄lb live mussels or cooked mussels in their shells, scrubbed carefully and rinsed thoroughly
350g/12oz dried maccheroncini or spaghetti
60ml/4 tbsp olive oil
2 garlic cloves, finely chopped
45ml/3 tbsp chopped fresh parsley
400g/14oz chopped and seeded ripe tomatoes, drained
sea salt and ground black pepper

1 If using fresh mussels, check and discard any that are not tightly closed, or that do not snap shut when tapped on the work surface.

2 Place the cleaned mussels in a wide frying pan. Cover the pan and place over medium-high heat for 5–6 minutes, shaking the pan frequently, until the mussels have opened. Any mussels that have not opened should be discarded. Remove all the mussels from the open shells, wipe off any traces of sand or sediment, and set them aside. Discard the shells.

3 Bring a pan of lightly salted water to the boil and cook the pasta according to the packet instructions. Meanwhile, heat the oil in a large frying pan and add the garlic and parsley. Fry for 5 minutes, then add the tomatoes. Season, stir, and cook over high heat for about 8 minutes. Stir in the mussels.

4 Drain the cooked pasta and add it to the pan containing the mussels and tomatoes. Stir well to coat the pasta in the sauce, then serve in warmed bowls.

Nutritional information per portion: Energy 452kcal/1910kJ; Protein 18.1g; Carbohydrate 68.3g, of which sugars 6.3g; Fat 13.8g, of which saturates 2g; Cholesterol 15mg; Calcium 128mg; Fibre 4.2g; Sodium 95mg.

Vermicelli with clam sauce

This recipe takes its name from the city of Naples, where both fresh tomato sauce and seafood are traditionally served with vermicelli. Here the two are combined to make a very tasty dish.

SERVES 4

1kg/2¼lb fresh clams, scrubbed thoroughly, discarding any that are open or do not close when sharply tapped

250ml/8fl oz/1 cup dry white wine

2 garlic cloves, bruised

1 large handful fresh flat leaf parsley, finely chopped

30ml/2 tbsp olive oil

1 small onion, finely chopped

8 ripe Italian plum tomatoes, peeled, seeded and finely chopped

½–1 fresh red chilli, seeded and finely chopped

350g/12oz dried vermicelli, cooked according to the packet instructions

salt and ground black pepper

1 Pour the wine into a large pan, add the garlic cloves and half the parsley, then the clams. Cover and bring to the boil over high heat. Cook for 5 minutes, shaking the pan, until the clams have opened.

2 Strain the clams over a bowl. Leave the clams until cool, then remove about two-thirds of them from their shells, pouring the clam liquor into the bowl of cooking liquid. Discard any clams that have failed to open. Set the clams aside, keeping the unshelled clams warm in a bowl covered with a lid.

3 Heat the oil in a pan, add the onion and cook gently, stirring for about 5 minutes until softened and lightly coloured. Add the tomatoes, then strain in the clam cooking liquid. Add the chilli and season. Bring to the boil, half-cover the pan and simmer for 15–20 minutes.

4 Add the shelled clams to the tomato sauce, stir and heat through gently for 2–3 minutes. Pour the sauce over the cooked pasta and toss together well. Garnish with the reserved clams, sprinkle the parsley over the pasta and serve.

Nutritional information per portion: Energy 504kcal/2109kJ; Protein 25.2g; Carbohydrate 76.8g, of which sugars 6g; Fat 7g, of which saturates 1.1g; Cholesterol 67mg; Calcium 129mg; Fibre 2.1g; Sodium 1226mg.

Seafood conchiglie

This is a very special modern dish, a warm salad composed of scallops, pasta and fresh rocket flavoured with roasted pepper, chilli and balsamic vinegar. It makes an impressive dish.

SERVES 4

8 large fresh scallops
300g/11oz/2¾ cups dried conchiglie
15ml/1 tbsp olive oil
15g/½ oz/1 tbsp butter
120ml/4fl oz/½ cup dry white wine
90g/3½oz rocket (arugula) leaves,
   stalks trimmed
salt and ground black pepper

FOR THE VINAIGRETTE

60ml/4 tbsp extra virgin olive oil
15ml/1 tbsp balsamic vinegar
1 piece bottled roasted (bell) pepper,
   drained and finely chopped
1–2 fresh red chillies, seeded
   and chopped
1 garlic clove, crushed
5–10ml/1–2 tsp clear honey,

1 Cut each scallop into 2–3 pieces. If the corals are attached, pull them off and cut each piece in half. Season the scallops and corals.

2 To make the vinaigrette, put the oil, vinegar, chopped pepper and chillies in a jug (pitcher) with the garlic and honey and whisk well.

3 Cook the pasta according to the instructions on the packet. Meanwhile, heat the oil and butter in a non-stick frying pan until sizzling.

4 Add half the scallops and toss over high heat for 2 minutes. Remove with a slotted spoon and keep warm. Cook the remaining scallops in the same way. Add the wine to the liquid left in the pan and stir over high heat until the mixture has reduced to a few tablespoons.

5 Drain the pasta and transfer to a bowl. Add the rocket, scallops, the reduced cooking juices and the vinaigrette and toss well to combine. Serve.

Nutritional information per portion: Energy 485kcal/2039kJ; Protein 18.4g; Carbohydrate 59.3g, of which sugars 4.9g; Fat 18.9g, of which saturates 4.3g; Cholesterol 26mg; Calcium 71mg; Fibre 2.7g; Sodium 126mg.

Risotto and pizza

The risotto and pizza dishes in this section are simple to make but substantial enough to provide a nutritious and filling meal, using fresh ingredients that all the family will enjoy. A creamy mushroom or shellfish risotto makes a divine main course, and pizzas, the ultimate convenience food, are always a firm family favourite.

Pumpkin, rosemary and chilli risotto

This rich and creamy risotto is made with arborio or vialone nano rice. The pumpkin speckles the rice with orange; the rosemary gives it a sweet pungency, while garlic and chilli add bite.

SERVES 4

115g/4oz/½ cup butter

1 small onion, finely chopped

2 large garlic cloves, crushed

1 fresh red chilli, seeded and finely chopped

250g/9oz fresh pumpkin or butternut squash, peeled and roughly chopped

30ml/2 tbsp chopped fresh rosemary

250g/9oz/1½ cups risotto rice, preferably arborio or vialone nano

about 750ml/1¼ pints/3 cups hot chicken stock, preferably fresh

50g/2oz/⅔ cup freshly grated Parmesan cheese, plus extra to serve

salt and ground black pepper

1 Melt half the butter in a heavy pan, add the onion and garlic, and cook for 10 minutes until softening. Add the chilli and cook for about 1 minute. Add the pumpkin or squash and cook, stirring constantly, for 5 minutes. Stir in the rosemary.

2 Add the rice, and stir with a wooden spoon to coat with the oil and vegetables. Cook for 2–3 minutes to toast the rice grains.

3 Begin to add the stock, a large ladleful at a time, stirring all the time until each ladleful has been absorbed into the rice. The rice should always be bubbling slowly. If not, add some more stock. Continue adding the stock like this, until the rice is tender and creamy, but the grains remain firm, and the pumpkin is beginning to disintegrate. (This should take about 20 minutes, depending on the type of rice used.) Taste and season well.

4 Stir the remaining butter and the Parmesan cheese into the rice. Cover and let the risotto rest for 2–3 minutes, then serve immediately with extra Parmesan cheese.

Nutritional information per portion: Energy 512kcal/ 2144kJ; Protein 10g; Carbohydrate 58g, of which sugars 2g; Fat 28g, of which saturates 17g; Cholesterol 73mg; Calcium 163mg; Fibre 1.9g; Sodium 666mg.

Risotto with spring vegetables

This is one of the prettiest risottos, especially if you can get yellow courgettes, but if you can't find yellow ones, use green ones. Asparagus tips can be used in place of the green beans.

SERVES 4

150g/5oz/1 cup shelled fresh peas

115g/4oz/1 cup green beans, cut into
    short lengths

30ml/2 tbsp olive oil

75g/3oz/6 tbsp butter

2 small yellow courgettes (zucchini), cut
    into matchsticks

1 onion, finely chopped

275g/10oz/1¹/₂ cups risotto rice

120ml/4 fl oz/¹/₂ cup Italian dry
    white vermouth

about 1 litre/1³/₄ pints/4 cups boiling
    chicken stock

75g/3oz/1 cup grated Parmesan cheese

a small handful of fresh basil leaves,
    finely shredded, plus a few whole
    leaves, to garnish

salt and ground black pepper

1 Blanch the peas and beans in a large pan of lightly salted boiling water for 2–3 minutes until just tender. Drain, refresh under cold running water, drain again and set aside.

2 Heat the oil and 25g/1oz/2 tbsp of the butter in a medium pan until foaming. Add the courgettes and cook gently for 2–3 minutes or until just softened. Remove with a slotted spoon and set aside. Add the onion to the pan and cook gently for about 3 minutes, stirring until it is softened.

3 Stir in the rice until the grains start to swell and burst, then add the vermouth. Stir until the vermouth stops sizzling and most of it has been absorbed by the rice, then add a few ladlefuls of the stock, with salt and pepper to taste. Stir over low heat until the stock has been absorbed.

4 Continue cooking and stirring for 20–25 minutes, adding the remaining stock a few ladlefuls at a time. The rice should be *al dente* and the risotto should have a moist and creamy appearance.

5 Gently stir in the vegetables, the remaining butter and about half the grated Parmesan. Heat through, then stir in the shredded basil and taste for seasoning. Garnish with a few whole basil leaves and serve hot, with the remaining grated Parmesan handed separately.

Nutritional information per portion: Energy 355kcal/ 1467kJ; Protein 12g; Carbohydrate 10g, of which sugars 5g; Fat 30g, of which saturates 15g; Cholesterol 57mg; Calcium 244mg; Fibre 3.2g; Sodium 944mg.

Oven-baked porcini risotto

This simple risotto is very easy to make because you do not have to stand over it stirring constantly as it cooks, as you do with a traditional risotto, and it is just as delcious.

SERVES 4

25g/1oz/¹/₂ cup dried porcini
    mushrooms, soaked in boiling water
    for 30 minutes
30ml/2 tbsp garlic-infused olive oil
1 onion, finely chopped
225g/8oz/generous 1 cup risotto rice
salt and ground black pepper

1 Drain the mushrooms through a sieve (strainer) lined with kitchen paper, reserving the soaking liquor. Rinse the mushrooms thoroughly under running water to remove any grit, and dry on kitchen paper.

2 Preheat the oven to 180°C/350°F/ Gas 4. Heat the oil in a roasting pan on the hob and add the finely chopped onion.

3 Cook for 2–3 minutes, or until softened. Add the rice and stir for 1–2 minutes. Add the mushrooms. Pour in the mushroom liquor and mix. Season and cover with foil.

4 Bake for 30 minutes, stirring occasionally, until all the stock has been absorbed and the rice is tender. Divide between warm serving bowls and serve immediately.

Nutritional information per portion: Energy 260kcal/1085kJ; Protein 4.8g; Carbohydrate 46.2g, of which sugars 0.9g; Fat 5.9g, of which saturates 0.8g; Cholesterol 0mg; Calcium 16mg; Fibre 0.5g; Sodium 2mg.

Shellfish risotto

Most supermarkets now stock packs of ready-prepared mixed shellfish, such as prawns, squid and mussels, which are ideal for making this quick risotto.

SERVES 4

1 litre/1³/4 pints/4 cups fish
   or shellfish stock
50g/2oz/¹/4 cup butter
2 shallots, chopped
2 garlic cloves, chopped
350g/12oz/1³/4 cups risotto rice
150ml/¹/4 pint/²/3 cup dry white wine
2.5ml/¹/2 tsp powdered saffron, or a
   pinch of saffron threads
400g/14oz mixed prepared shellfish
30ml/2 tbsp freshly grated
   Parmesan cheese
30ml/2 tbsp chopped fresh
   flat leaf parsley, to garnish
salt and ground black pepper

1 Pour the fish or shellfish stock into a large pan. Bring it to the boil, then reduce the heat and keep it at a gentle simmer. The water needs to be hot when it is added to the rice.

2 Melt the butter in a pan, add the shallots and garlic and cook over low heat until soft. Add the rice, stir well to coat the grains with butter, then pour in the wine. Cook over medium heat, stirring occasionally, until all the wine has been absorbed.

3 Add a ladleful of hot stock and the saffron and cook, stirring constantly, until the liquid has been absorbed. Add the shellfish and stir well. Continue to add stock a ladleful at a time, waiting until each quantity has been absorbed.

4 Stir for 20 minutes, until the rice is creamy, but still with a little bite in the middle. Mix in the Parmesan cheese and season. Sprinkle over the chopped parsley and serve.

Nutritional information per portion: Energy 404kcal/1693kJ; Protein 28.1g; Carbohydrate 56.3g, of which sugars 1.1g; Fat 3.9g, of which saturates 1.9g; Cholesterol 228mg; Calcium 200mg; Fibre 0.2g; Sodium 301mg.

Pancetta and broad bean risotto

Risottos are a great way of using up leftover ingredients, and this one makes a healthy and filling meal. Serve with cooked fresh seasonal vegetables or a fresh mixed green salad.

SERVES 4

15ml/1 tbsp olive oil

1 onion, chopped

2 garlic cloves, finely chopped

175g/6oz smoked pancetta, diced

350g/12oz/1¾ cups risotto rice

1.2 litres/2 pints/5 cups chicken stock

225g/8oz frozen baby broad (fava) beans

30ml/2 tbsp chopped fresh mixed herbs,
     such as parsley, thyme and oregano

salt and ground black pepper

shavings of Parmesan cheese, to serve

chopped fresh flat leaf parsley,
     to garnish

1 Heat the oil in a large pan or frying pan. Add the onion, garlic and pancetta and cook gently for about 5 minutes, stirring occasionally.

2 Add the risotto rice to the pan and cook for 1 minute, stirring. Add 300ml/½ pint/1¼ cups of the stock and simmer, stirring frequently until the stock has been absorbed.

3 Continue adding the stock, a ladleful at a time, stirring frequently until the rice is *al dente* and creamy, and almost all the liquid has been absorbed. This will take 30–35 minutes. It may not be necessary to add all the stock.

4 Meanwhile, cook the broad beans in a pan of lightly salted, boiling water for about 3 minutes until tender. Drain and keep warm.

5 Stir the beans, mixed herbs and seasoning into the risotto. Serve sprinkled with shavings of Parmesan cheese and garnished with chopped parsley.

Nutritional information per portion: Energy 485kcals/2031kJ; Protein 22.35g; Carbohydrate 74.7g, of which sugars 1.93g; Fat 9.9g, of which saturates 1.7g; Cholesterol 0mg; Calcium 00mg; Fibre 4.36g; Sodium 1969mg.

Classic margherita pizza

A margherita pizza makes a lovely simple supper, but of course you can add any extra toppings you like. Prosciutto and rocket make a great addition – just add them after it is cooked.

SERVES 2

half a 300g/11oz packet pizza base mix
45ml/3 tbsp ready-made tomato and
   basil sauce
150g/5oz mozzarella, sliced
15ml/1 tbsp herb-infused
   olive oil
salt and ground black pepper

1 Make the pizza base mix according to the instructions on the packet. Brush the base with a little of the olive oil and spread over the tomato and basil sauce, not quite to the edges.

2 Arrange the slices of mozzarella on top of the pizza and bake for about 25–30 minutes, or until the edges are golden.

3 Drizzle the remaining oil on top of the pizza, season with salt and black pepper and serve immediately, garnished with fresh basil leaves.

Nutritional information per portion: Energy 420kcal/1761kJ; Protein 7.6g; Carbohydrate 49.8g, of which sugars 7.8g; Fat 22.6g, of which saturates 2.2g; Cholesterol 2mg; Calcium 133mg; Fibre 3.4g; Sodium 130mg.

Butternut squash and sage pizza

The combination of the sweet butternut squash, sage and sharp goat's cheese works wonderfully on this pizza. Pumpkin and winter squashes are popular in northern Italy.

SERVES 4

15g/½oz/1 tbsp butter
30ml/2 tbsp olive oil
2 shallots, finely chopped
1 butternut squash, peeled, seeded
    and cubed, about 450g/1lb
    prepared weight
16 sage leaves
1 quantity Pizza Dough, *see* page 84
1 quantity Basic Tomato Sauce,
    see page 211
115g/4oz/1 cup mozzarella cheese, sliced
115g/4oz/½ cup firm goat's cheese
salt and ground black pepper

1 Preheat the oven to 200°C/400°F/Gas 6. Oil four baking sheets. Put the butter and oil in a roasting pan and heat in the oven for a few minutes. Add the shallots, squash and half the sage leaves. Toss to coat. Roast for 15–20 minutes until tender. Raise the oven temperature to 220°C/425°F/Gas 7.

2 Divide the pizza dough into four pieces and roll out each piece on a lightly floured surface to a 25cm/10in round. Transfer each round to a baking sheet and spread with the tomato sauce, leaving a 1cm/½in border all around. Spoon the squash and shallot mixture over the top.

3 Arrange the slices of mozzarella over the squash mixture and crumble the goat's cheese over. Sprinkle the remaining sage leaves over and season. Bake for 15–20 minutes until the cheese has melted and the crust is golden.

Nutritional information per portion: Energy 771kcal/ 3243kJ; Protein 26g; Carbohydrate 102g, of which sugars 13g; Fat 32g, of which saturates 12g; Cholesterol 45mg; Calcium 451mg; Fibre 5.2g; Sodium 1330mg.

Ricotta and fontina pizza

The flavour combination of the earthy mixed mushrooms are delicious with the creamy ricotta and fontina cheeses and makes an excellent pizza topping that the family will enjoy.

SERVES 4

FOR THE PIZZA DOUGH
2.5ml/½ tsp active dried yeast
pinch of sugar
450g/1lb/4 cups strong white bread flour
5ml/1 tsp salt
30ml/2 tbsp olive oil

FOR THE TOMATO SAUCE
400g/14oz can chopped tomatoes
150ml/¼ pint/⅔ cup passata
1 large garlic clove, finely chopped
5ml/1 tsp dried oregano
1 bay leaf
10ml/2 tsp malt vinegar
salt and ground black pepper

FOR THE TOPPING
30ml/2 tbsp olive oil
1 garlic clove, finely chopped
350g/12oz/4 cups mixed mushrooms brown cap (cremini),
    field (portabello) or button (white), sliced
30ml/2 tbsp chopped fresh oregano,
    plus whole leaves, to garnish
250g/9oz/generous 1 cup ricotta cheese
225g/8oz Fontina cheese, sliced

1 Make the dough. Put 300 ml/½ pint/1¼ cups warm water in a measuring cup. Add the yeast and sugar and leave for 5–10 minutes until frothy.

2 Sift the flour and salt into a bowl and make a well in the centre. Gradually pour in the yeast mixture and the olive oil. Mix to make a smooth dough.

3 Knead on a lightly floured surface for about 10 minutes until smooth, springy and elastic. Place the dough in a floured bowl, cover and leave to rise in a warm place for 1½ hours.

4 Meanwhile, make the tomato sauce. Place all the ingredients in a pan, cover and bring to the boil. Lower the heat, remove the lid and simmer for 20 minutes, stirring occasionally, until reduced.

5 Make the topping. Heat the oil in a frying pan. Add the chopped garlic and mushrooms, and season to taste with salt and pepper. Cook, stirring, for about 5 minutes or until the mushrooms are tender and golden. Set aside.

6 Preheat the oven to 220°C/425°F/Gas 7. Brush four baking sheets with oil. Knead the dough for about 2 minutes, then divide into four equal pieces. Roll out each piece to a 25cm/10in round and place on a baking sheet.

7 Spoon the tomato sauce over each dough round leaving a 1cm/½in border all around. Brush the edge with a little olive oil. Add the mushrooms, oregano and cheese. Bake for about 15 minutes until golden brown and crisp. Sprinkle over the oregano leaves.

Nutritional information per portion: Energy 851kcal/ 3572kJ; Protein 36g; Carbohydrate 90g, of which sugars 6g; Fat 41g, of which saturates 18g; Cholesterol 79mg; Calcium 78mg; Fibre 7.0g; Sodium 1219mg.

Fiorentina pizza

An egg adds the finishing touch to this spinach and red onion-topped pizza; try not to overcook it however, as it is at its best when the yolk is still slightly soft in the middle. Calzone is made in the same way as this pizza, but is folded in half to conceal the filling. Add the egg with the rest of the pizza topping, fold over the dough, seal the edges and bake for 20 minutes.

SERVES 2–3

45ml/3 tbsp olive oil
1 small red onion, thinly sliced
175g/6oz fresh spinach, stalks removed
1 pizza base, about 25–30cm/10–12in diameter
½ quantity Basic Tomato Sauce (*see* p.211)

freshly grated nutmeg
150g/5oz mozzarella cheese
1 egg
25g/1oz/¼ cup Gruyère cheese, grated

1 Heat 15ml/1 tbsp of the oil and fry the onion until soft. Add the spinach and fry until wilted. Drain any excess liquid.

2 Preheat the oven to 220°C/425°F/Gas 7. Brush the pizza base with half the remaining olive oil.

3 Using the back of a spoon spread the pizza sauce evenly over the base leaving a 1cm/½in border all around the edges.

4 Top with the spinach mixture. Sprinkle over a little freshly grated nutmeg.

5 Thinly slice the mozzarella and arrange over the spinach. Drizzle over the remaining oil. Bake for 10 minutes, then remove from the oven.

6 Make a small well in the centre of the pizza topping and carefully break the egg into the hole.

7 Sprinkle over the grated Gruyère cheese and return to the oven for a further 5–10 minutes until crisp and golden. Serve immediately.

Nutritional information per portion: Energy 503kcal/2100kJ; Protein 20.8g; Carbohydrate 40.3g, of which sugars 5.9g;
Fat 29.7g, of which saturates 10.9g; Cholesterol 101mg; Calcium 417mg; Fibre 2.9g; Sodium 668mg.

Mozzarella and ham pizza with rocket

This home-made pizza uses a combination of smoked cheese and ham on a bed of onions, with a thin and crispy base. The rocket is thrown on top to wilt into the cheese.

SERVES 2–4

75ml/5 tbsp olive oil
1kg/2¼lb onions, finely sliced
15ml/1 tbsp chopped fresh rosemary
10ml/2 tsp dried oregano
115g/4oz sliced smoked ham, torn into pieces
1 smoked mozzarella, peeled and thinly sliced
30ml/2 tbsp freshly grated Parmesan cheese
100g/4oz rocket (arugula)
salt and ground black pepper

FOR THE PIZZA DOUGH
25g/1oz fresh yeast, 15g/½oz dried active baking yeast
**   or 2 sachets easy-blend (rapid-rise) dried yeast**
a pinch of sugar
350g/12oz/3 cups Italian "00" flour, plus extra,
**   for dusting**
30ml/2 tbsp olive oil, plus extra for brushing
**   and drizzling**
5ml/1 tsp salt

1 To make the dough, cream the fresh yeast with the sugar in a medium bowl and whisk in 250ml/8fl oz/1 cup warm water. Leave for 10 minutes until frothy. If using another type of yeast, follow the manufacturer's instructions.

2 Sift the flour into a bowl and make a well in the centre. Pour in the yeast mixture, olive oil and salt. Mix together with a round-bladed knife, then use your hands to form a soft dough. Transfer the dough to a lightly floured surface and knead for 10 minutes until smooth and elastic. Place in a clean, oiled bowl, cover with a damp dish towel and leave to rise for about 1 hour until doubled in bulk.

3 To make the pizza topping, heat the oil in a pan and add the onions. Cook over gentle heat until the onions are soft and golden. Stir in the herbs and season with salt and pepper.

4 Preheat the oven to 240°C/475°F/Gas 9. Knock back (punch down) the pizza dough. Divide the dough in half and roll out to make two rounds 25–30cm/10–12in in diameter, and about 5mm/¼in thick. Slide these on to two well-floured, flat baking sheets.

5 Cover the pizza bases with the onions, ham and mozzarella on top. Sprinkle with the Parmesan cheese. Bake in the oven for 15 minutes until golden and crisp. Pile the rocket on top and serve.

Nutritional information per portion: Energy 804kcal/ 3362kJ; Protein 30g; Carbohydrate 87g, of which sugars 16g; Fat 40g, of which saturates 11g; Cholesterol 24mg; Calcium 426mg; Fibre 8.0g; Sodium 1380mg.

Fried pizza pasties

These tasty little morsels are served all over central and southern Italy as a snack food or as part of a hot antipasti selection. Although similar to calzone they are fried instead of baked.

SERVES 4

Ingredients
½ **quantity Pizza Dough,**
    see **page 84**
½ **quantity Basic Tomato Sauce,**
    see **page 211**
225g/8oz **mozzarella cheese,**
    chopped
115g/4oz **Italian salami,**
    thinly sliced
handful of fresh basil leaves,
    roughly torn
sunflower oil, for deep frying

1 Preheat the oven to 200°C/400°F/ Gas 6. Brush two baking sheets with oil. Divide the dough into 12 and roll out each piece on a lightly floured surface to a 10cm/4in round.

2 Spread the centre of each round with a little of the tomato sauce, leaving sufficient border all round for sealing the pasty, then top with a few pieces of mozzarella and salami slices.

3 Sprinkle with salt and ground black pepper and add a few fresh basil leaves to each round. Brush the edges of the dough rounds with a little water, then fold over and press together to seal.

4 Heat oil to a depth of about 10cm/4in in a pan. When hot, deep-fry the pasties, a few at a time, for 8–10 minutes until golden. Drain on kitchen paper and serve hot.

Nutritional information per portion: Energy 602kcal/ 2516kJ; Protein 24g; Carbohydrate 45g, of which sugars 4g; Fat 37g, of which saturates 14g; Cholesterol 56mg; Calcium 297mg; Fibre 2.5g; Sodium 1078mg.

Sicilian pizza

This robustly flavoured pizza is topped with mozzarella and Pecorino cheeses. For best results choose olives that have been marinated in olive oil with herbs and garlic.

SERVES 2

1 small aubergine (eggplant), cut into
    thin rounds
30ml/2 tbsp olive oil
1/2 quantity risen Pizza Dough,
    see page 84
1/2 quantity Basic Tomato Sauce,
    see page 211
175g/6oz mozzarella cheese, sliced
50g/2oz/1/2 cup stoned (pitted)
    black olives
15ml/1 tbsp drained capers
60ml/4 tbsp grated Pecorino cheese
salt and ground black pepper

1 Preheat the oven to 200°C/400°F/ Gas 6. Brush one or two baking sheets with oil. Brush the aubergine rounds with olive oil and arrange them on the baking sheet(s).

2 Bake for 10–15 minutes, turning once, until browned and tender. Remove the aubergine slices from the baking sheet(s) and drain on kitchen paper.

3 Raise the oven temperature to 220°C/425°F/Gas 7.

4 Roll out the pizza dough to two 25cm/10in rounds. Transfer to baking sheets and spread with the tomato sauce.

5 Pile the aubergine slices on top of the tomato sauce and cover with the sliced mozzarella. Dot with the black olives and capers. Sprinkle the Pecorino cheese liberally over the top, and season with plenty of salt and pepper. Bake for 15–20 minutes until the crust on each pizza is golden in colour.

Nutritional information per portion: Energy 969kcal/ 4062kJ; Protein 40g; Carbohydrate 93g, of which sugars 10g; Fat 51g, of which saturates 20g; Cholesterol 69mg; Calcium 727mg; Fibre 8.9g; Sodium 2427mg.

Hot pepperoni pizza

There is nothing more mouthwatering than a freshly baked pizza, especially when the topping includes thin slices of pepperoni, dried oregano and sizzling red chillies.

SERVES 6

225g/8oz/2 cups strong white
    bread flour
2 tsp easy-blend (rapid-rise) dried yeast
1 tsp sugar
1/2 tsp salt
1 tbsp olive oil
175ml/6 fl oz/3/4 cup mixed
    hand-hot milk and water

TOPPING
400g/14oz can chopped tomatoes, well drained
2 garlic cloves, crushed
1 tsp dried oregano
225g/8oz mozzarella cheese, coarsely grated
2 dried red chillies, crumbled
225g/8oz pepperoni, sliced
2 tbsp drained capers
fresh oregano, to garnish

1 Sift the flour into a bowl. Stir in the yeast, sugar and salt. Make a well in the centre. Stir the olive oil into the milk and water, then stir the mixture into the flour. Mix to a soft dough.

2 Knead the dough on a lightly floured surface for 5–10 minutes until it is smooth and elastic. Return it to the clean, lightly oiled, bowl and cover with clear film (plastic wrap). Leave in a warm place for about 30 minutes or until the dough has doubled in bulk. Preheat the oven to 220°C/425°F/Gas 7.

3 Turn the dough out on to a lightly floured surface and knead lightly for about 1 minute. Divide the dough in half and roll each piece out to a 25cm/10in circle. Place on lightly oiled pizza trays or baking sheets. To make the topping, mix the drained tomatoes, garlic and oregano in a bowl.

4 Spread half the mixture over each round, leaving a margin around the edge. Set half the mozzarella aside. Divide the rest between the pizzas. Bake for 7–10 minutes until the dough rim on each pizza is pale golden.

5 Sprinkle the crumbled chillies over the pizzas, then arrange the pepperoni slices and capers on top. Sprinkle with the remaining mozzarella, then return the pizzas to the oven and bake for 7–10 minutes more. Sprinkle over the oregano and serve immediately.

Nutritional information per portion: Energy 631kcal/2640kJ; Protein 28.8g; Carbohydrate 47.6g, of which sugars 4.7g;
Fat 37.6g, of which saturates 16.8g; Cholesterol 80mg; Calcium 318mg; Fibre 2.7g; Sodium 1499mg.

Salmon and avocado pizza

A mixture of smoked and fresh salmon makes a delicious pizza topping when mixed with avocado. Capers add a touch of piquancy to cut the richness of the major ingredients.

SERVES 3–4

150g/5oz salmon fillet
120ml/4fl oz/½ cup dry white wine
15ml/1 tbsp olive oil
400g/14oz can chopped tomatoes, drained
115g/4oz mozzarella cheese, grated
1 small avocado, halved, stoned (pitted),
    peeled and cubed
10ml/2 tsp lemon juice
30ml/2 tbsp crème fraîche or sour cream
75g/3oz smoked salmon, cut
    into strips

15ml/1 tbsp drained bottled capers
30ml/2 tbsp chopped fresh chives,
    to garnish
ground black pepper

FOR THE PIZZA BASE

175g/6oz/1½ cups strong white (bread) flour
1.5ml/¼ tsp salt
5ml/1 tsp easy-blend (rapid-rise) dried yeast
120–150ml/4–5fl oz/½–⅔ cup lukewarm water
15ml/1 tbsp olive oil

1 Make the pizza base. Sift the flour and salt into a mixing bowl, stir in the yeast, then make a well in the centre.

2 Add the lukewarm water to the well, then add the oil. Mix with a spoon, gradually incorporating the flour to make a soft dough.

3 Knead the dough until smooth and elastic, then place in a bowl, cover with clear film (plastic wrap) and leave in a warm place for about 1 hour or until the dough has doubled in bulk.

4 Knock back (punch down) the dough, knead it briefly, then roll it out to a 25–30cm/10–12in round and support on a baking sheet. Push up the edges of the dough a little to make a rim.

5 Preheat the oven to 220°C/425°F/Gas 7. Place the salmon in a frying pan, pour over the wine and season. Bring slowly to the boil, remove from the heat, cover and cool. (The fish will cook in the cooling liquid.) Skin and flake the salmon, removing any bones.

6 Brush the pizza base with the oil and spread over the drained tomatoes. Sprinkle over 50g/2oz of the mozzarella. Bake for 10 minutes. Meanwhile, toss the avocado in the lemon juice.

7 Dot teaspoonfuls of the crème fraîche or sour cream over the pizza base. Arrange the fresh and smoked salmon, avocado, capers and remaining mozzarella on top.

8 Season with black pepper. Bake for a further 10 minutes until crisp and golden. Sprinkle over the chives and serve immediately.

Nutritional information per portion: Energy 451kcal/1884kJ; Protein 22g; Carbohydrate 31g, of which sugars 5.3g;
Fat 25.3g, of which saturates 8.6g; Cholesterol 53mg; Calcium 193mg; Fibre 3.3g; Sodium 282mg.

Poultry, meat and game

The Italians eat a wide variety of different meats, according to region. Veal, pork and poultry are popular all over the country, while beef is farmed and eaten more in the north, and lamb is a great Roman speciality. All meats are eaten as a second course, and are usually served solo with a selection of delicious and seasonal vegetables to follow.

Chicken with chianti

Together the red wine and red pesto give this sauce a rich colour and a spicy flavour, while the grapes add a delicious sweetness. Serve the stew with grilled polenta or warm crusty bread, and accompany with a piquant salad, such as rocket or watercress, tossed in a dressing.

SERVES 4

45ml/3 tbsp olive oil
4 part-boned chicken breast portions, skinned
1 medium red onion
30ml/2 tbsp red pesto
300ml/1/2 pint/11/4 cups Chianti

300ml/1/2 pint/11/4 cups water
115g/4oz red grapes, halved lengthways and seeded if necessary
salt and ground black pepper
fresh basil leaves, to garnish
rocket (arugula) salad, to serve

1 Heat 30ml/2 tbsp of the oil in a large frying pan, add the chicken breast portions and sauté over medium heat for 5 minutes until they have changed colour on all sides. Remove with a slotted spoon and drain on kitchen paper.

2 Cut the onions in half, through the root. Trim off the root, then slice the onion halves lengthways to create thin wedges.

3 Heat the remaining oil in the pan, add the onion wedges and red pesto and cook gently, stirring constantly, for about 3 minutes until the onion is softened, but not browned.

4 Add the Chianti and water to the pan and bring to the boil, stirring, then return the chicken to the pan and add salt and pepper to taste.

5 Reduce the heat, then cover the pan and simmer over gentle head for about 20 minutes or until the chicken is tender, stirring occasionally.

6 Add the grapes to the pan and cook over low to medium heat until heated through, then season to taste. Serve the chicken hot, garnished with basil and accompanied by the rocket salad.

Nutritional information per portion: Energy 303kcal/ 1268kJ; Protein 32g; Carbohydrate 8g, of which sugars 7g; Fat 16g, of which saturates 3g; Cholesterol 91mg; Calcium 61mg; Fibre 0.8g; Sodium 211mg.

Chicken with prosciutto and cheese

There is nothing quite like the buttery texture and nutty taste of Fontina cheese.
It has superb melting qualities and is delicious grilled over chicken.

SERVES 4

2 thin slices of prosciutto
2 thin slices of Fontina cheese
4 part-boned chicken quarters
4 sprigs of basil
30ml/2 tbsp olive oil
15g/¹⁄₂ oz/1 tbsp butter
120ml/4 fl oz/¹⁄₂ cup dry white wine
salt and ground black pepper
tender young salad leaves, to serve

1 Preheat the oven to 200°C/400°F/Gas 6. Lightly oil a baking dish. Cut the prosciutto and Fontina slices in half crossways. Skin the chicken portions, open out a slit in the centre of each one, and fill each cavity with half a ham slice and a basil sprig.

2 Heat the oil and butter in a wide frying pan until foaming. Cook the chicken portions over medium heat for 1–2 minutes on each side until they change colour. Transfer to the baking dish. Add the wine to the pan juices, stir until sizzling, then pour over the chicken and season to taste.

3 Top each chicken portion with a slice of Fontina. Bake for 20 minutes or until the chicken is tender. Serve hot, with tender young salad leaves.

Nutritional information per portion: Energy 263kcal/ 1097kJ; Protein 32g; Carbohydrate 0g, of which sugars 0g; Fat 15g, of which saturates 5g; Cholesterol 103mg; Calcium 4.7mg; Fibre 0g; Sodium 315mg.

Devilled chicken

It is clear that this spicy, barbecued chicken dish comes from southern Italy because it has dried red chillies in the marinade. Versions without the chillies are just as good.

SERVES 4

120ml/4 fl oz/½ cup olive oil

finely grated rind and juice of
   1 large lemon

2 garlic cloves, finely chopped

10ml/2 tsp finely chopped or crumbled
   dried red chillies

12 skinless, boneless chicken thigh
   portions, each cut into 3 or 4 pieces

salt and ground black pepper

flat leaf parsley leaves, to garnish

lemon wedges, to serve

1 Make a marinade by mixing the oil, lemon rind and juice, garlic and chillies in a large, shallow glass or ceramic dish. Add salt and pepper to taste. Whisk well, then add the chicken portions, turning to coat with the marinade. Cover and marinate in the refrigerator for at least 4 hours, or preferably overnight.

2 When ready to cook, preheat the grill (broiler) and thread the chicken portions on to eight oiled metal skewers. Cook under a hot grill (broiler) for about 6–8 minutes, turning frequently, until tender. Garnish with parsley leaves and serve hot, with lemon wedges for squeezing.

Nutritional information per portion: Energy 456kcal/ 1892kJ; Protein 26g; Carbohydrate 1g, of which sugars 1g; Fat 39g, of which saturates 7g; Cholesterol 132mg; Calcium 17mg; Fibre 0g; Sodium 41mg.

Chicken in the style of macerata

This recipe of chicken slow-cooked with livers is named after the city of Macerata, although similar versions appear on the menu in other parts of Tuscany. After two hours of cooking, the chicken is wonderfully moist, tender and full of flavour.

SERVES 4–6

200g/7oz chicken giblets
15g/¹⁄₂oz/1 tbsp unsalted butter
90ml/6 tbsp extra virgin olive oil
1 oven-ready free-range chicken,
    about 3kg/6lb 9oz
chicken stock, as needed

3 eggs, beaten
juice and grated rind of ¹⁄₂ large,
    unwaxed lemon
sea salt
handful chopped fresh flat leaf parsley
    and lemon slices, to garnish

1 Clean and trim all the giblets and chop them coarsely. Put them in a deep pan with a lid over medium heat and add the butter and olive oil. Cook together for 5 minutes. Lay the chicken in the pan and cook the chicken briefly on all sides to seal.

2 Pour in an even mixture of water and chicken stock to come about three-quarters of the way up the pan. Add salt and cover tightly, then simmer gently for about 1¹⁄₂–2 hours, or until the chicken is cooked through.

3 The liquid in the pan should have almost completely evaporated. Take the chicken out of the pan and carve it into portions. Arrange the carved chicken on a warmed serving dish.

4 Whisk together the eggs and the juice and rind of the lemon, then add to the juices left in the pan. Beat until the eggs thicken slightly.

5 Pour this sauce over the chicken portions, sprinkle with parsley and serve immediately, garnished with lemon slices.

Nutritional information per portion: Energy 765kcal/3174kJ; Protein 64.1g; Carbohydrate 0g, of which sugars 0g; Fat 56.3g, of which saturates 17.1g; Cholesterol 421mg; Calcium 40mg; Fibre 0g; Sodium 304mg.

Pork ribs with mushrooms and artichokes

The rough-textured sauce served with the ribs comes from the high Sila mountain of Calabria. It uses preserved mushrooms and carciofi (artichokes), which is very fitting, considering that the area is famous for bottling and salting these regional products, or preserving them in oil.

SERVES 4

400g/14oz can plum tomatoes in tomato juice
60ml/4 tbsp olive oil
12 fresh basil leaves, coarsely shredded
50g/2oz/¹⁄₂ cup preserved mushrooms
   in olive oil

50g/2oz/¹⁄₂ cup preserved artichoke hearts
   in olive oil
8 pork rib chops
sea salt and ground black pepper

1 Drain the canned tomatoes, reserving the juice. Remove the seeds and chop the tomatoes roughly.

2 Heat the oil in a pan and add the tomatoes. Fry over medium heat for 15 minutes, stirring frequently and adding a little of the reserved juice if necessary to prevent the mixture from sticking to the pan.

3 Season with salt and pepper and add the basil leaves. Simmer for 15 minutes more, stirring from time to time.

4 Preheat the grill (broiler) or prepare a barbecue. Chop the mushrooms and the artichoke hearts finely.

5 Add the chopped mushrooms and artichokes, with most of their oil, to the tomato sauce. Stir well and leave the sauce over a low heat while you cook the rib chops.

6 Place the chops on a rack under the hot grill. Cook for 2 minutes on each side, then lower the heat and cook for 8 minutes more or until done to your liking.

7 Divide the chops among four warmed plates, put the sauce in a bowl, and serve immediately.

Nutritional information per portion: Energy 484kcal/2012kJ; Protein 29g; Carbohydrate 3.2g, of which sugars 3.1g; Fat 39.7g, of which saturates 10.6g; Cholesterol 99mg; Calcium 30mg; Fibre 1.1g; Sodium 157mg.

Porchetta

This is a simplified version of a traditional Italian festive dish. Make sure the piece of belly pork has a good amount of crackling – because this is the best part, which guests will love. Serve with creamy mashed potatoes and a green vegetable.

SERVES 8

2kg/4¹/₂lb boned pork belly
45ml/3 tbsp fresh rosemary leaves,
  roughly chopped
50g/2oz/²/₃ cup freshly grated
  Parmesan cheese
15ml/1 tbsp olive oil
salt and ground black pepper
mashed potatoes and green
  vegetables, to serve (optional)

1 Preheat the oven to 180°C/350°F/ Gas 4. Lay the pork belly skin side down on a board. Spread the rosemary leaves over the meat and sprinkle with the grated cheese. Season, and drizzle over the olive oil.

2 Starting from one end, roll the pork up firmly and tie string around it at 2.5cm/1in intervals, to secure.

3 Transfer the rolled pork to a roasting pan and cook for about 3 hours, or until cooked through.

4 Transfer the cooked pork to a carving board and leave to rest for 10 minutes, then carve into slices. Serve immediately with the mashed potatoes and green vegetables if you like.

Nutritional information per portion: Energy 604kcal/ 2511kJ; Protein 50g; Carbohydrate 0g, of which sugars 0g; Fat 45g, of which saturates 16g; Cholesterol 176mg; Calcium 102mg; Fibre 0g; Sodium 260mg.

Roast lamb with figs

Lamb fillet is an expensive cut of meat, but because it is so lean there is very little waste.
To make a more economical version of this dish, use leg of lamb instead. It has a stronger
flavour but is equally good. Serve with steamed green beans.

SERVES 4

30ml/2 tbsp olive oil
1kg/2¹/₄lb lamb fillet
9 fresh figs
150ml/¹/₄ pint/²/₃ cup ruby port
salt and ground black pepper
steamed green beans, to serve
   (optional)

1 Preheat the oven to 190°/375°F/ Gas 5. Heat the oil in a roasting pan over medium heat. Add the lamb fillet and sear on all sides until evenly browned.

2 Cut the figs in half and arrange around the lamb. Season the lamb and roast for 30 minutes. Pour the port over the figs.

3 Return the lamb to the oven and roast for a further 30–45 minutes until the middle is slightly pink.

4 Transfer the cooked lamb to a carving board and leave to rest for about 5 minutes. Carve the meat into thick slices and divide among individual dishes. Serve with steamed green beans, if you like.

Nutritional information per portion: Energy 527kcal/2213kJ; Protein 35.2g; Carbohydrate 39.5g, of which sugars 39.5g; Fat 23.5g, of which saturates 9.2g; Cholesterol 127mg; Calcium 187mg; Fibre 5.2g; Sodium 187mg.

Pot-roasted shoulder of lamb

This delicious boned and rolled shoulder of lamb, studded with rosemary sprigs and garlic, then cooked on a bed of vegetables, makes a perfect alternative to a traditional roast.

SERVES 6

15ml/1 tbsp olive oil

1.3kg/3lb lamb shoulder, trimmed, boned and tied

3 large garlic cloves, cut into quarters

12 small fresh rosemary sprigs

115g/4oz lean rinded smoked bacon, chopped

1 onion, chopped

3 carrots, finely chopped

3 celery sticks, finely chopped

1 leek, finely chopped

150ml/¼ pint/⅔ cup red wine

300ml/½ pint/1¼ cups lamb or vegetable stock

400g/14oz can chopped tomatoes

3 sprigs of fresh thyme

2 bay leaves

400g/14oz can flageolet (small cannellini) beans, drained and rinsed

salt and ground black pepper

cooked potatoes or warm crusty bread, to serve (optional)

1 Heat the oil in a large frying pan and brown the lamb on all sides. Remove from the pan and leave to stand until it is cool enough to handle. When the lamb is cool enough, make twelve deep incisions all over the meat. Push a piece of garlic and a small sprig of rosemary into each incision.

2 Add the bacon, onion, carrots, celery and leek to the pan and cook for about 10 minutes until soft, then transfer to the cooking pot. Stir the red wine into the cooking pot. Add the stock and chopped tomatoes to the pot and season with salt and pepper. Add the thyme and bay leaves, submerging them in the liquid. Place the lamb on top, cover with the lid and cook on high for 4 hours.

3 Lift the lamb out of the pot and stir the beans into the vegetable mixture. Return the lamb, re-cover and cook for a further 1–2 hours, or until the lamb is cooked and tender. Remove the cooked lamb from the cooking pot, cover with foil to keep warm, and leave to rest for 10 minutes.

4 Remove the string from the lamb and carve the meat into thick slices. Remove the thyme and bay leaves from the vegetable and bean mixture and carefully skim off any fat from the surface. Spoon the vegetables on to warmed serving plates and arrange the sliced lamb on top. Serve with cooked potatoes or warm crusty bread if you like.

Nutritional information per portion: Energy 554kcal/ 2308kJ; Protein 47g; Carbohydrate 18g, of which sugars 7g; Fat 36g, of which saturates 15g; Cholesterol 150mg; Calcium 53mg; Fibre 4.4g; Sodium 589mg.

Beef stew with tomatoes, wine and peas

It seems there are as many recipes for stews as there are Italian cooks. Stufato di manzo is very traditional. Serve it with boiled or mashed potatoes to soak up the deliciously rich sauce.

SERVES 4

30ml/2 tbsp plain (all-purpose) flour

10ml/2 tsp chopped fresh thyme or
   5ml/1 tsp dried thyme

1 kg/2¼lb braising or stewing steak,
   cut into large cubes

45ml/3 tbsp olive oil

1 medium onion, roughly chopped

450g/1lb jar sugocasa or passata
   (bottled strained tomatoes)

250ml/8fl oz/1 cup beef stock

250ml/8fl oz/1 cup red wine

2 garlic cloves, crushed

30ml/2 tbsp tomato paste

275g/10oz/2 cups shelled fresh peas

5ml/1 tsp sugar

salt and ground black pepper

fresh thyme, to garnish

1 Preheat the oven to 160°C/325°F/Gas 3. Put the flour in a dish and season with the thyme and salt and pepper. Add the beef and coat evenly.

2 Heat the oil in a large flameproof casserole, add the beef and brown on all sides over a medium to high heat. Remove and drain on kitchen paper.

3 Add the onion to the pan, scraping the base of the pan to mix in any sediment. Cook gently for about 3 minutes, stirring frequently, until softened, then stir in the sugocasa or passata, stock, wine, garlic and tomato paste. Bring to the boil, stirring. Return the beef to the pan and stir well to coat with the sauce. Cover and cook in the oven for 1½ hours.

4 Stir in the peas and sugar. Return the casserole to the oven and cook for 30 minutes more, or until the beef is tender. Taste for seasoning. Garnish with fresh thyme before serving.

Nutritional information per portion: Energy 518kcal/ 2167kJ; Protein 63g; Carbohydrate 20g, of which sugars 7g; Fat 21g, of which saturates 5g; Cholesterol 168mg; Calcium 58mg; Fibre 4.1g; Sodium 420mg.

Meatballs with peperonata

A classic from southern Italy, this tasty stew with meatballs is classic Italian fare, and is a popular dish all over the world. This version goes extremely well with creamed potatoes.

SERVES 4

400g/14oz minced (ground) beef
115g/4oz/2 cups white breadcrumbs
50g/2oz/²/₃ cup grated Parmesan cheese
2 eggs, beaten
pinch of paprika
pinch of grated nutmeg
5ml/1 tsp dried mixed herbs
2 thin slices of mortadella, chopped
vegetable oil, for shallow frying
salt and ground black pepper
snipped fresh basil leaves, to garnish

FOR THE PEPERONATA

30ml/2 tbsp olive oil
1 small onion, thinly sliced
2 yellow and 2 red (bell) peppers,
    cored, seeded and cut lengthways
    into thin strips
275g/10oz/1¹/₄ cups passata
15ml/1 tbsp chopped fresh parsley

1 Mix the minced beef in a bowl with half the breadcrumbs and all the remaining ingredients, and season well.

2 Divide the mixture into 12 equal balls, flattening each the slightly so they are about 1cm/¹/₂in thick. Put the remaining breadcrumbs on a plate and roll the meatballs in them, until they are evenly coated. Place on a plate, cover with clear film (plastic wrap) and chill for about 30 minutes to firm up.

3 Meanwhile, make the peperonata. Heat the oil in a pan, add the onion and cook gently for about 3 minutes, stirring, until softened. Add the pepper strips and cook for 3 minutes, stirring. Stir in the passata and parsley, and season. Bring to the boil, cover and cook for 15 minutes, then remove the lid and continue to cook until reduced and thick. Taste for seasoning. Keep hot.

4 Pour oil into a frying pan and shallow fry the meatballs for 10–12 minutes, turning them 3–4 times and pressing them flat. Remove and drain on kitchen paper. Serve hot, with the peperonata. Garnish with the basil.

Nutritional information per portion: Energy 518kcal/ 2166kJ; Protein 34g; Carbohydrate 25g, of which sugars 11g; Fat 32g, of which saturates 10g; Cholesterol 119mg; Calcium 207mg; Fibre 2.9g; Sodium 594mg.

Tuscan pot roast

This hearty pot roast is delicious served with plenty of red wine. It is cooked over a low heat for about 6 hours, which gives wonderfully tender beef and a rich stock for a tasty sauce.

SERVES 4

1.5kg/3¼lb beef brisket in a
   single piece
2–3 garlic cloves, cut into long strips
50g/2oz fatty pancetta, chopped
75g/3oz/6 tbsp unsalted butter
1 onion, chopped
1 carrot, chopped
1 celery stick, chopped
1 litre/1¾ pints/4 cups simmering
   beef stock
15ml/1 tbsp tomato paste
sea salt and ground black pepper

1 Pierce the meat all over with a knife and insert strips of garlic to taste.

2 Put a large flameproof casserole over medium heat and add the pancetta, butter, onion, carrot and celery. Fry together for about 8 minutes, stirring constantly. Add the meat and seal it on all sides.

3 Pour over about 300ml/½ pint/1¼ cups stock, season with salt and pepper and stir in the tomato paste. Cover and simmer over a very low heat for about 6 hours, adding more stock occasionally to prevent the casserole from drying out. When the meat is tender and cooked through, remove it from the casserole and set it aside to keep warm.

4 Strain the vegetables and stock left in the casserole, and season to taste. Slice the meat thickly and arrange it on a warmed platter. Pour over the sieved (strained) sauce and serve.

Nutritional information per portion: Energy 707kcal/2955kJ; Protein 81.7g; Carbohydrate 2.7g, of which sugars 2.3g; Fat 41.2g, of which saturates 20.6g; Cholesterol 254mg; Calcium 30mg; Fibre 0.7g; Sodium 537mg.

Florentine T-bone steak

This recipe is almost the symbol of Florentine gastronomy: a luscious, rare and tender steak of beef, grilled over a wood fire and dressed simply with oil, rosemary, garlic, and salt and pepper.

SERVES 4

3–4 rosemary sprigs
3–4 garlic cloves
30–45ml/2–3 tbsp extra virgin olive oil
1 T-bone steak, about 675g/1½lb
sea salt and ground black pepper
simple salad and crusty bread to serve, (optional)

1 Bruise the rosemary and garlic by bashing them lightly with a rolling pin.

2 Place the bruised rosemary and garlic in a flat dish, then add the olive oil. Stir to mix, then add the steak and leave to marinate for 24–48 hours.

3 Light the barbecue and, when the flames have died down, position the grill rack over the hot coals. Cook the steak to taste. Alternatively, preheat a grill (broiler) to high, then cook the steak for 2 minutes on each side for medium-rare, or 3–4 minutes for well-done. Serve with a simple salad and crusty bread, if you like.

Nutritional information per portion: Energy 1008kcal/4182kJ; Protein 83.1g; Carbohydrate 0.7g, of which sugars 0.6g; Fat 74.5g, of which saturates 28.3g; Cholesterol 236mg; Calcium 74mg; Fibre 1.3g; Sodium 154mg.

Osso bucco with risotto milanese

Osso bucco, literally meaning 'bone with a hole', is a traditional Milanese stew of veal, onions and leeks in white wine. Many of today's versions also include tomatoes. Risotto Milanese is the archetypal Italian risotto and the classic accompaniment for osso bucco.

SERVES 4

50g/2oz/¼ cup butter
15ml/1 tbsp olive oil
1 large onion, chopped
1 leek, finely chopped
45ml/3 tbsp plain (all-purpose) flour
4 large portions of veal shin, hind cut
600ml/1 pint/2½ cups dry white wine
salt and ground black pepper

FOR THE RISOTTO
25g/1oz/2 tbsp butter
1 onion, finely chopped

350g/12oz/1⅔ cups risotto rice
1 litre/1¾ pints/4 cups boiling
   chicken stock
2.5ml/½ tsp saffron strands
60ml/4 tbsp white wine
50g/2oz/⅔ cup Parmesan cheese,
   coarsely grated

FOR THE GREMOLATA
grated rind of 1 lemon
30ml/2 tbsp chopped fresh parsley
1 garlic clove, finely chopped

1 Heat the butter and oil until sizzling in a large frying pan. Add the onion and leek, and cook gently for about 5 minutes without browning the onions.

2 Season the flour and toss the veal in it, then add the pieces to the pan and cook over a high heat until they brown.

3 Gradually stir in the wine and heat until simmering. Cover the pan and simmer for 1½ hours, stirring occasionally, or until the meat is very tender. Use a slotted spoon to transfer the veal to a warm serving dish, then boil the sauce rapidly until reduced and thickened to the required consistency.

4 Make the risotto about 30 minutes before the end of the cooking time for the stew. Melt the butter in a large pan and cook the onion until softened.

5 Stir in the rice to coat all the grains in butter. Add a ladleful of boiling chicken stock and mix well. Continue adding the boiling stock a ladleful at a time, allowing each portion to be absorbed before adding the next. The whole process takes about 20 minutes.

6 Pound the saffron strands in a mortar and pestle, then slowly stir in the white wine with the saffron. Add the saffron-scented wine to the risotto and cook for a final 5 minutes. Remove the pan from the heat and stir in the Parmesan.

7 Mix the lemon rind, parsley and garlic for the gremolata. Spoon some risotto on to each plate, then add some veal. Sprinkle with gremolata and serve immediately.

Nutritional information per portion: Energy 901kcal/3764kJ; Protein 49.1g; Carbohydrate 92g, of which sugars 8g; Fat 25.9g, of which saturates 13.7g; Cholesterol 130mg; Calcium 248mg; Fibre 2.9g; Sodium 349mg.

Traditional rabbit casserole

Rabbit is a much-loved meat in most parts of Italy. Stufato di coniglio is a truly ancient recipe, although the method also works with jointed chicken. Serve with polenta or roast potatoes.

SERVES 8–10

2 rabbits, about 900g/2lb each, each cut into five pieces

90ml/6 tbsp strong red or white wine vinegar

6 garlic cloves, peeled

3 large rosemary sprigs

2.5ml/¹/₂ tsp sea salt

2.5ml/¹/₂ tsp ground black pepper

75ml/2¹/₂fl oz/¹/₃ cup olive oil

750ml/1¹/₄ pints/3 cups red wine

15ml/1 tbsp tomato paste

1 Put the rabbit joints into a bowl. Mix the wine vinegar with 600ml/ 1 pint/2¹/₂ cups water and pour over the rabbit. Soak for 1 hour.

2 Drain the rabbit joints and dry them carefully on kitchen paper. Chop half the garlic cloves and one rosemary sprig and mix them with the salt and pepper. Rub this mixture all over the rabbit joints.

3 Chop the remaining garlic. Heat the oil in a large pan and add the garlic and remaining rosemary. Fry the rabbit joints all over until brown. Add the red wine gradually, so that it simmers constantly.

4 Stir in the tomato paste and 300ml/¹/₂ pint/1¹/₄ cups hot water. Cover and simmer gently for 45 minutes, until cooked. Serve.

Nutritional information per portion: Energy 265kcal/1106kJ; Protein 25.2g; Carbohydrate 0.4g, of which sugars 0.4g; Fat 12.5g, of which saturates 3.7g; Cholesterol 124mg; Calcium 17mg; Fibre 0g; Sodium 40mg.

Wild boar cacciatora

Cinghiale, or wild boar, is synonymous with Italian cuisine. In the forests and mountains this wild animal has long been prized for its excellent meat. Serve with cooked spinach.

SERVES 6

45ml/3 tbsp extra virgin olive oil

2 onions, thickly sliced

2 celery sticks, thickly sliced

2 carrots, thickly sliced

900g/2lb wild boar meat, cut into
    large chunks

about 500ml/17fl oz/2¹/₄ cups
    dry red wine

1 large rosemary sprig

FOR THE CACCIATORA SAUCE

75ml/5 tbsp extra virgin olive oil

1 garlic clove, crushed

¹/₂ large onion, chopped

1 dried red chilli

300ml/¹/₂ pint/1¹/₄ cups Basic
    Tomato Sauce, *see* page 211

sea salt

cooked spinach, to serve (optional)

1 Put the oil in a pan and fry the onions, celery and carrots for 10–15 minutes, or until well browned.

2 Meanwhile, place the wild boar chunks in a deep bowl. Pour in the wine and add the rosemary and vegetables. The wine should cover the meat completely; add more wine if necessary and mix together. Leave to marinate overnight.

3 Drain and dry the meat, reserving the marinade. In a non-stick pan, brown all the meat.

4 Once the meat has released its liquid, remove and set it aside. Discard the liquid left in the pan.

5 To make the cacciatora sauce, add the oil to the pan with the garlic, onion and chilli. Fry together for 5 minutes, stirring, then pour over the tomato sauce. Season with salt and simmer gently for 10 minutes.

6 Add the meat to the sauce. Lower the heat, cover and simmer for 1 hour, or until tender. Serve with spinach, if you like.

Nutritional information per portion: Energy 430kcal/1791kJ; Protein 33.8g; Carbohydrate 7.5g, of which sugars 4.7g; Fat 23.5g, of which saturates 5.1g; Cholesterol 100mg; Calcium 39mg; Fibre 1.5g; Sodium 294mg.

Fish and shellfish

Italy has such an extensive coastline –

and so many lakes, rivers and streams

– that it is no small wonder that fish

and shellfish are so popular. Of course

there are many different types that are

unique to the country itself, but the

most common varieties are available

outside Italy. Cooking methods are

very simple and quick, and any sauces

are light and fresh.

Pan-fried sole with lemon

The delicate flavour and texture of sole is brought out in this simple, classic recipe. Lemon sole is used here because it is easier to obtain – and is less expensive – than Dover sole.

SERVES 2

30–45ml/2–3 tbsp plain
   (all-purpose) flour
4 lemon sole fillets
45ml/3 tbsp olive oil
50g/2oz/¹⁄₄ cup butter
60ml/4 tbsp lemon juice
30ml/2 tbsp rinsed bottled capers
salt and ground black pepper
fresh flat leaf parsley and lemon
   wedges, to garnish

1 Season the flour with salt and black pepper. Coat the sole fillets evenly on both sides. Heat the oil with half the butter in a large pan until foaming. Add two sole fillets and fry over medium heat for 2–3 minutes on each side.

2 Lift out the sole fillets with a fish slice and place on a warmed serving platter. Keep hot. Fry the remaining sole fillets.

3 Remove the pan from the heat and add the lemon juice and the rest of the butter. Return the pan to high heat and stir until the pan juices are sizzling and turn golden brown. Remove from the heat and stir in the capers.

4 Pour the pan juices over the sole, sprinkle with salt and pepper to taste and garnish with the parsley. Add the lemon wedges and serve immediately.

Nutritional information per portion: Energy 425kcal/1773kJ; Protein 34.2g; Carbohydrate 5.9g, of which sugars 0.2g; Fat 29.7g, of which saturates 9.3g; Cholesterol 111mg; Calcium 103mg; Fibre 0.3g; Sodium 316mg.

Monkfish with tomato and olive sauce

This dish comes from the coast of Calabria in southern Italy. Garlic-flavoured mashed potato is delicious with the robust tomato and olive sauce.

SERVES 4

450g/1lb fresh mussels, scrubbed

a few fresh basil sprigs

2 garlic cloves, roughly chopped

300ml/½ pint/1¼ cups dry
   white wine

30ml/2 tbsp olive oil

15 g/½ oz/1 tbsp butter

900g/2lb monkfish fillets, skinned and
   cut into large chunks

1 onion, finely chopped

500g/1¼lb jar passata (bottled
   strained tomatoes)

15ml/1 tbsp sun-dried tomato paste

115g/4oz/1 cup stoned (pitted)
   black olives

salt and ground black pepper

extra fresh basil leaves, to garnish

garlic-flavoured mashed potatoes, to
   serve (optional)

1 Put the mussels in a pan with a few basil leaves, the garlic and wine. Bring to the boil, then simmer for 5 minutes, shaking the pan frequently. Remove the mussels, discarding any that fail to open. Strain the liquid and reserve.

2 Heat the oil and butter until foaming, add the monkfish pieces and sauté over medium heat until they just change colour, then remove from the heat. Add the onion to the juices in the pan and cook gently for 5 minutes, stirring until softened. Add the passata, the reserved cooking liquid from the mussels and the tomato paste. Season to taste. Bring to the boil, stirring, then lower the heat, cover and simmer for 20 minutes, stirring occasionally.

3 Pull off and discard the top shells from the mussels. Add the monkfish pieces to the tomato sauce and cook gently for 5 minutes. Stir in the olives and remaining basil, then season. Place the mussels in their half-shells on top of the sauce, cover the pan and heat the mussels through for 1–2 minutes. Serve immediately with mashed potatoes, if using, garnished with basil.

Nutritional information per portion: Energy 375kcal/ 1580kJ; Protein 52g; Carbohydrate 12g, of which sugars 8g; Fat 14g, of which saturates 2g; Cholesterol 78mg; Calcium 103mg; Fibre 1.7g; Sodium 1212mg.

Three-colour fish kebabs with salsa

Do not let the fish marinate for more than an hour for this dish. The lemon juice will start to break down the fibres of the fish after this time and it will be difficult not to overcook it.

SERVES 6

120ml/4 fl oz/½ cup olive oil
finely grated rind and juice of 1 large lemon
5ml/1 tsp crushed chilli flakes
350g/12oz monkfish fillet, cubed
350g/12oz swordfish fillet, cubed
350g/12oz thick salmon fillet or steak, cubed
2 red, yellow or orange (bell) peppers, cored,
    seeded and cut into squares
30ml/2 tbsp finely chopped fresh
    flat leaf parsley
salt and ground black pepper

**FOR THE SWEET TOMATO
AND CHILLI SALSA**

225g/8oz ripe tomatoes, finely chopped
1 garlic clove, crushed
1 fresh red chilli, seeded and chopped
45ml/3 tbsp extra virgin olive oil
15ml/1 tbsp lemon juice
15ml/1 tbsp finely chopped fresh
    flat leaf parsley
pinch of sugar

1 Put the oil in a shallow glass or ceramic bowl and add the lemon rind and juice, the chilli flakes and pepper to taste. Whisk to combine, then add the fish chunks. Turn to coat evenly.

2 Add the pepper squares, stir, then cover and marinate in a cool place for 1 hour, turning occasionally.

3 Preheat the grill (broiler). Thread the fish and peppers on to eight oiled metal skewers, reserving the marinade. Grill (broil) the skewered fish for 5–8 minutes, turning once.

4 Meanwhile, make the salsa by mixing all the ingredients in a large bowl, and season to taste with plenty of salt and pepper. Heat the reserved marinade in a small pan, remove from the heat and stir in the chopped parsley, with salt and pepper to taste. Serve the fish kebabs hot, with the marinade spooned over, accompanied by the salsa.

Nutritional information per portion: Energy 498kcal/ 2071kJ; Protein 33g; Carbohydrate 9g, of which sugars 8g; Fat 37g, of which saturates 6g; Cholesterol 61mg; Calcium 37mg; Fibre 2.8g; Sodium 189mg.

Grilled red mullet with rosemary

This classic Italian recipe is very simple – the taste of grilled triglia (red mullet) is so good in itself that it needs very little to bring out the exquisite flavour of the fish.

SERVES 4

4 red mullet or snapper, cleaned, about
   275g/10oz each
4 garlic cloves, cut lengthways into
   thin slivers
75ml/5 tbsp olive oil
30ml/2 tbsp balsamic vinegar
10ml/2 tsp fresh rosemary, very finely
   chopped, or 5ml/1 tsp dried rosemary
ground black pepper
sea salt, to serve
fresh rosemary sprigs and lemon wedges,
   to garnish

1 Cut three diagonal slits in both sides of each fish. Push the garlic slivers into the slits. Place the fish in a single layer in a shallow dish. Whisk the oil, vinegar and rosemary, with ground black pepper to taste.

2 Pour the oil and vinegar mixture over the fish, cover with clear film (plastic wrap) and leave to marinate in a cool place for about 1 hour. Remove from the marinade, and grill (broil) each fish for 5–6 minutes on each side, turning once and brushing with the marinade.

3 Serve hot, sprinkled with sea salt and garnished with fresh rosemary sprigs, with lemon wedges for squeezing over.

Nutritional information per portion: Energy 268kcal/ 1112kJ; Protein 16g; Carbohydrate 1g, of which sugars 0g; Fat 22g, of which saturates 3g; Cholesterol 0mg; Calcium 64mg; Fibre 0g; Sodium 83mg.

Roast sea bass

Sea bass has wonderfully meaty flesh. It can be quite an expensive fish, and is best cooked as simply as possible. Avoid elaborate sauces, which would mask its delicate texture.

SERVES 4

1 fennel bulb with fronds, about 275g/10oz
120ml/4fl oz/½ cup olive oil
1 small red onion, diced
2 sea bass, about 500g/1¼lb each, cleaned with heads left on
4 lemon slices, and extra to garnish (optional)
juice of 2 lemons
120ml/4fl oz/½ cup dry white wine
salt and ground black pepper

1 Preheat the oven to 190°C/375°F/Gas 5. Cut the fronds off the top of the fennel and reserve. Cut the bulb lengthways into thin slices, then dice. Heat 30ml/2 tbsp of the oil in a frying pan, add the diced fennel and onion, and cook gently, stirring for 5 minutes until softened. Remove from the heat.

2 Make three diagonal slashes on both sides of each sea bass. Brush a roasting pan generously with oil, add the fish and tuck two lemon slices in each cavity. Sprinkle the softened fennel and onion over the fish.

3 Whisk the remaining oil and the lemon juice and season, then pour over the fish. Cover with foil and roast for 30 minutes, removing the foil for the last 10 minutes. Discard the lemon slices, transfer the fish to a dish. Keep hot.

4 Put the roasting pan on top of the stove. Add the wine and stir over medium heat to incorporate all the pan juices. Bring to the boil, then spoon over the fish. Garnish with the reserved fennel fronds and lemon slices.

Nutritional information per portion: Energy 386kcal/ 1598kJ; Protein 20g; Carbohydrate 3g, of which sugars 3g; Fat 33g, of which saturates 5g; Cholesterol 80mg; Calcium 153mg; Fibre 0.3g; Sodium 176mg.

Calabrian tuna steaks

This recipe typifies Calabrian cuisine and brings together many foods that are closely identified with the region. The ingredients work very well together, making the most of the taste of fresh tuna and creating a satisfying dish, with just enough chilli to add a hint of fire.

SERVES 4

4 evenly sized fresh tuna steaks,
   total weight about 800g/1¾lb
60ml/4 tbsp olive oil
30ml/2 tbsp plain (all-purpose) flour
60ml/4 tbsp dry white wine

FOR THE SAUCE
50g/2oz pancetta, chopped
1 large garlic clove, chopped

1 onion, chopped
30ml/2 tbsp chopped fresh parsley
4 anchovy fillets in oil, drained
   and boned
400g/14oz can chopped tomatoes,
   drained
½ dried red chilli, chopped
sea salt and ground black pepper

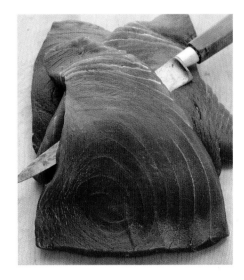

1 Rinse the tuna steaks in cold water, drain and pat dry. Season the steaks thoroughly on both sides with salt and pepper.

2 Heat half the olive oil in a frying pan large enough to hold the tuna steaks in a single layer. Coat the steaks lightly in flour, add them to the pan and fry them over medium heat for 3 minutes on each side.

3 Sprinkle with the wine and allow the alcohol to boil off for 1 minute. Lift out the cooked fish and drain on kitchen paper. Place on a plate and spoon over the pan juices.

4 To make the sauce, heat the remaining oil in the pan. Add the pancetta, garlic, onion and half the parsley. Fry gently for 5 minutes.

5 Add the anchovy fillets and mash them into the hot sauce mixture with a fork. After 1 minute, stir in the tomatoes. Add the chilli and simmer over a very low heat for 15 minutes.

6 Slide the tuna steaks back into the pan and spoon some of the tomato mixture over them. Heat through thoroughly for about 8 minutes, turning them over gently once. Serve the tuna immediately, topped with the sauce and sprinkled with the remaining parsley.

Nutritional information per portion: Energy 472kcal/1976kJ; Protein 51.7g; Carbohydrate 10.2g, of which sugars 4.2g; Fat 24.2g, of which saturates 5.1g; Cholesterol 64mg; Calcium 64mg; Fibre 1.5g; Sodium 380mg.

Marinated eels

In the many rivers and slow-moving streams of the Italian plains, eels are caught and turned into delicious, simple dishes for the table. This is a recipe from the Pisa area, and it is served cold.

SERVES 4

900g/2lb very fresh eels

coarse sea salt, for cleaning

150ml/¼ pint/⅔ cup extra virgin
   olive oil

3 garlic cloves

1 dried red chilli

3 fresh sage leaves

1 rosemary sprig

300ml/½ pint/1¼ cups white
   wine vinegar

sea salt

1 Clean the outside of the eels carefully to remove all trace of slime, using coarse sea salt. Split and gut them, then wash and dry them. Cut into finger-length chunks.

2 Heat the oil in a frying pan and fry the eel chunks until golden brown all over. Remove them with a slotted spoon and drain on kitchen paper. Place in a bowl to cool.

3 Using the same oil, fry the garlic, chilli, sage and rosemary together for 3 minutes. Add the white wine vinegar to the frying pan and then boil to reduce by about one-third. Season with salt.

4 Pour this marinade over the eels and cover the bowl. Leave to marinate for about 48 hours before serving.

Nutritional information per portion: Energy 603kcal/2499kJ; Protein 37.4g; Carbohydrate 0g, of which sugars 0g; Fat 50.4g, of which saturates 10g; Cholesterol 338mg; Calcium 43mg; Fibre 0g; Sodium 200mg.

Jailed octopus

The sweet taste of octopus makes it a much sought-after ingredient. The name of this recipe has arisen because the octopus is traditionally cooked in a tightly sealed pot until tender.

SERVES 6

800g/1³/4lb tiny octopuses or squid
100ml/3¹/2fl oz/scant ¹/2 cup extra
   virgin olive oil
2 garlic cloves, chopped
a handful of fresh flat leaf parsley
   leaves, chopped
sea salt and ground black pepper

1 Clean the octopuses or squid carefully, removing eyes, beaks and bladders. Wash thoroughly in salted water. Peel the cleaned octopuses or squid and cut into small chunks.

2 Put the oil in a large pan and fry the garlic over low heat for 5 minutes, or until soft.

3 Add the octopuses or squid to the pan. Season with plenty of salt and pepper, and cover with a lid.

4 Simmer for 30 minutes, or until the octopuses or squid are tender, shaking the pan from time to time to prevent sticking. Add the fresh parsley and serve piping hot.

Nutritional information per portion: Energy 212kcal/888kJ; Protein 24.1g; Carbohydrate 0.2g, of which sugars 0.2g; Fat 12.8g, of which saturates 1.9g; Cholesterol 64mg; Calcium 61mg; Fibre 0.4g; Sodium 3mg.

Stuffed squid

In Italy, it is usual for cooks to use just a few basic, but good-quality, ingredients. The squid for this dish must be fresh and carefully cleaned, and the tomatoes need to be juicy and sweet.

SERVES 4

60ml/4 tbsp olive oil

1 garlic clove, crushed

9 tomatoes, peeled and seeded

4 large squid, cleaned and ready
   to cook

60ml/4 tbsp dry breadcrumbs

60ml/4 tbsp grated Pecorino cheese

1 egg, beaten

sea salt and ground black pepper

chopped fresh parsley, to garnish

1 Heat the olive oil in a wide, shallow pan that is large enough to hold all the squid in one layer. Add the garlic and fry over medium heat for 5 minutes. Do not let it burn or it will taste bitter.

2 Chop the tomatoes, then add them to the pan. Season with salt and pepper to taste. Bring to the boil, then lower the heat and simmer for 30 minutes, stirring frequently and adding a little water if the sauce becomes dry.

3 Chop the squid tentacles and add them to the sauce. Remove from the heat and set aside while you make the stuffing.

4 Put the breadcrumbs in a bowl and add the cheese and enough of the beaten egg to bind the mixture. Mix the stuffing well.

5 Spoon the stuffing into the squid, dividing it evenly among them. The mixture will swell during cooking, so do not overfill the squid.

6 Either sew the stuffed squid closed using a darning needle threaded with fine cooking string (twine), or secure them with wooden cocktail sticks (toothpicks).

7 Lower the stuffed squid into the sauce, cover the pan and simmer very gently for about 1½ hours or until the squid are very tender, adding more water as required.

8 Season with salt and pepper, then serve either hot or cold, garnished with parsley, with crusty bread and a fresh green salad.

Nutritional information per portion: Energy 418kcal/1758kJ; Protein 37.7g; Carbohydrate 20.7g, of which sugars 7.4g; Fat 21.2g, of which saturates 5.9g; Cholesterol 456mg; Calcium 245mg; Fibre 2.6g; Sodium 508mg.

Chargrilled squid

If you like your food hot, add some – or all – of the chilli seeds with the flesh. If not, cut the chillies in half lengthways, scrape out the seeds and discard them.

SERVES 2

2 whole squid, with tentacles, cleaned
   and ready to cook
75ml/5 tbsp olive oil
30ml/2 tbsp balsamic vinegar
2 fresh red chillies, finely chopped
60ml/4 tbsp dry white wine
salt and ground black pepper
cooked risotto rice, hot, to serve
sprigs of fresh parsley, to garnish

1 Make a lengthways cut down the body of each squid, then open out the body flat. Score the flesh on both sides in a criss-cross pattern. Chop the tentacles. Place all the squid in a dish. Whisk the oil and vinegar in a bowl. Season and pour over the squid. Cover and marinate for 1 hour.

2 Heat a ridged pan until hot. Add the body of one of the squid. Cook over medium heat for 2–3 minutes, pressing the squid with a fish slice to keep it flat. Repeat on the other side. Cook the other squid body in the same way.

3 Cut the squid bodies into diagonal strips. Place the hot risotto rice in the centre of plates and top with the strips of squid. Keep hot.

4 Add the tentacles and chillies to the pan and cook over medium heat for 2 minutes. Stir in the wine, then add to the squid and rice. Garnish with parsley.

Nutritional information per portion: Energy 502kcal/ 2087kJ; Protein 31g; Carbohydrate 12g, of which sugars 0g; Fat 41g, of which saturates 6g; Cholesterol 450 mg; Calcium 27mg; Fibre 0g; Sodium 417mg.

Pan-fried prawns in their shells

Although expensive, this is a very quick and simple dish, ideal for an impromptu Italian supper with friends. Serve with hot crusty bread to scoop up the juices.

SERVES 4

60ml/4 tbsp extra virgin olive oil

32 large fresh prawns (shrimp),
   in their shells

4 garlic cloves, finely chopped

120ml/4 fl oz/¹/₂ cup Italian dry
   white vermouth

45ml/3 tbsp passata (bottled
   strained tomatoes)

salt and ground black pepper

fresh flat leaf parsley, chopped,
   to garnish

crusty bread, to serve

1 Heat the olive oil in a large frying pan until just sizzling. Add the prawns and toss over medium to high heat until their shells just begin to turn pink.

2 Sprinkle the garlic over the prawns in the pan and toss again, then add the vermouth and let it bubble, tossing the prawns constantly so that they cook evenly and absorb the flavours of the garlic and vermouth.

3 Keeping the pan on the heat, add the passata, with salt and pepper to taste. Stir until the prawns are thoroughly coated in the sauce. Serve immediately, sprinkled with the parsley and accompanied by plenty of hot crusty bread.

Nutritional information per portion: Energy 186kcal/ 775kJ; Protein 11g; Carbohydrate 1g, of which sugars 1g; Fat 15g, of which saturates 2g; Cholesterol 126mg; Calcium 54mg; Fibre 0g; Sodium 832mg.

Stuffed mussels with tomato sauce

This is a very tasty way to enjoy fresh mussels. Use the biggest shellfish you can find, as the preparation is more fiddly if the mussels are small. Clean them carefully, as any trace of grit or splinter of barnacle will spoil the effect of the whole dish.

SERVES 4

1kg/2¼lb live mussels, scrubbed and bearded
75ml/5 tbsp olive oil
3 garlic cloves
600ml/l pint/2½ cups passata
   (bottled strained tomatoes) or sieved
   (strained) canned tomatoes

2 eggs, beaten
30ml/2 tbsp chopped fresh parsley
120ml/8 tbsp soft white breadcrumbs
a small handful of fresh basil,
   leaves torn into shreds
sea salt and ground black pepper

1 Check the mussels, discarding any with damaged shells and any which are open and fail to close when tapped on the work surface.

2 Spread out the mussels in a wide frying pan. Cover the pan and place it over fairly high heat. Shake the pan frequently. After about 6 minutes, all the mussels should have opened and yielded their liquid. Discard any that remain closed. Drain the mussels, reserving the liquid in the pan, and set them aside.

3 Heat the oil in a medium pan. Peel 2 garlic cloves and add them, whole, to the oil. Fry the garlic until it turns brown, then lift the cloves out with a slotted spoon and discard them. Stir the passata or sieved tomatoes into the garlic-flavoured oil and season. Bring to the boil, then lower the heat, cover and simmer for 20 minutes.

4 Meanwhile, make the stuffing. Chop the remaining garlic clove finely and put it in a bowl. Add the eggs, parsley and breadcrumbs. Season with salt and pepper. Fill the empty half-shell of each mussel with the stuffing, then close the shells around the mussels. Tie each one with a loop of kitchen string (twine) to keep the stuffing securely inside.

5 Strain the reserved liquid from the mussels and add it to the tomato sauce, with the basil. Mix, then add the mussels to the pan and spoon the sauce over them. Cover and simmer for 10 minutes.

6 Remove the string from the mussels and transfer them, with the sauce, to a heated platter. Serve.

Nutritional information per portion: Energy 366kcal/1537kJ; Protein 21.2g; Carbohydrate 29g, of which sugars 6.5g; Fat 19.3g, of which saturates 3.1g; Cholesterol 125mg; Calcium 238mg; Fibre 3g; Sodium 441mg.

Insalata di mare

You can vary the fish in this Italian salad according to what is available, but try to include at least two kinds of shellfish and some squid. The salad is good warm or cold.

SERVES 4

450g/1lb fresh mussels, scrubbed and bearded

450g/1lb small clams, scrubbed

105ml/7 tbsp dry white wine

225g/8oz squid, cleaned

4 large scallops, with their corals

30ml/2 tbsp olive oil

2 garlic cloves, finely chopped

1 small dried red chilli, crumbled

225g/8oz whole cooked prawns (shrimp),
   in the shell

6–8 large chicory (Belgian endive) leaves

6–8 radicchio leaves

15ml/1 tbsp chopped flat leaf parsley, to garnish

FOR THE DRESSING

5ml/1 tsp Dijon mustard

30ml/2 tbsp white wine vinegar

5ml/1 tsp lemon juice

120ml/4fl oz/1/2 cup extra virgin olive oil

salt and ground black pepper

1 Put the mussels and clams in a large pan with the white wine. Cover and cook over high heat, shaking the pan occasionally, for 4 minutes, until they have opened. Discard any that remain closed. Use a slotted spoon to transfer them to a bowl, then strain and reserve the cooking liquid and set it aside.

2 Heat the oil in a frying pan. Cut the squid into thin rings; chop the tentacles. Leave small squid whole. Halve the scallops horizontally and add to the pan with the garlic, chilli and sauté for 2 minutes, until just cooked and tender. Lift the squid and scallops out, and reserve the oil. Leave the shellfish to cool.

3 Shell the cooled shellfish, keeping a dozen of each in the shell. Peel all but 6–8 of the prawns. Pour the shellfish cooking liquid into a small pan, set over high heat and reduce by half. Mix all the shelled and unshelled mussels and clams with the squid and scallops, then add the prawns.

4 To make the dressing, whisk the mustard with the vinegar and lemon juice and season to taste. Add the olive oil, whisk vigorously, then whisk in the reduced cooking liquid and the oil from the frying pan. Pour the dressing over the shellfish mixture and toss lightly to coat well.

5 Arrange the chicory and radicchio leaves around the edge of a serving dish and pile the mixed shellfish salad into the centre. Sprinkle with the chopped flat leaf parsley and serve.

Nutritional information per portion: Energy 445kcal/1861kJ; Protein 41.1g; Carbohydrate 3.7g, of which sugars 1g; Fat 27.9g, of which saturates 4.3g; Cholesterol 241mg; Calcium 219mg; Fibre 0.5g; Sodium 585mg.

Vegetarian dishes
and accompaniments

There is no shortage of fresh

vegetables in Italy, and the dishes are

imaginative and varied. Most Italian

cooks buy only when the vegetables

are in season and at their best, so you

will rarely find winter and summer

vegetables together in one dish. The

list of irresistible salad combinations is

endless, often with roasted ingredients

stirred into crisp green leaves.

Frittata with sun-dried tomatoes

A frittata is an Italian omelette and, similar to a Spanish omelette, it is cooked until firm enough to be cut into wedges and can be served hot, warm or cold.

SERVES 3–4

6 sun-dried tomatoes
60ml/4 tbsp olive oil
1 small onion, finely chopped
pinch of fresh thyme leaves
6 eggs
50g/2oz/²/₃ cup freshly grated
**   Parmesan cheese**
salt and ground black pepper
sprigs of thyme, to garnish
shavings of Parmesan, to serve

1 Cut a small cross in the top of each tomato then cover them with hot water. Soak for 15 minutes, then pat dry. Reserve the soaking water. Cut into strips.

2 Heat the oil in a pan. Add the onion and cook for 5 minutes, stir in the sun-dried tomatoes and thyme, and cook for 2–3 minutes. Season.

3 Break the eggs into a bowl and beat lightly. Stir in 45ml/3 tbsp of the tomato soaking water and the Parmesan. Increase the heat.

4 When the oil is sizzling, add the eggs. Mix quickly into the other ingredients. Lower the heat and cook for 4–5 minutes, until golden.

5 Take a large plate, place it upside down over the pan and, holding it firmly with oven gloves, turn the pan and the frittata over on to it.

6 Slide the frittata back into the pan, and cook for 3–4 minutes more until golden. Remove from the heat. Cut the frittata into wedges, garnish with sprigs of thyme and serve.

Nutritional information per portion: Energy 170kcal/705kJ; Protein 5.7g; Carbohydrate 3g, of which sugars 2.6g; Fat 15.2g, of which saturates 4.1g; Cholesterol 13mg; Calcium 158mg; Fibre 0.6g; Sodium 167mg.

Frittata with leek, red pepper and spinach

An alternative way to serve this frittata is to pack it into a hollowed-out loaf, drizzle it with olive oil, wrap tightly in clear film (plastic wrap) and chill for 1–2 hours before cutting into slices.

SERVES 3–4

30ml/2 tbsp olive oil

1 large red (bell) pepper, seeded and diced

2.5–5ml/¹/₂–1 tsp ground toasted cumin

3 leeks (about 450g/1lb), thinly sliced

150g/5oz small spinach leaves

45ml/3 tbsp pine nuts, toasted

5 large eggs

15ml/1 tbsp chopped fresh basil

15ml/1 tbsp chopped fresh flat leaf parsley

salt and ground black pepper

watercress or rocket (arugula), to garnish

50g/2oz Parmesan cheese, grated, to serve (optional)

1 Heat a frying pan and add the oil. Add the pepper and cook over medium heat, stirring for 6–8 minutes, until soft. Add 2.5ml/ ¹/₂ tsp of the cumin and cook for another 1–2 minutes.

2 Stir in the leeks, part-cover the pan and cook gently for 5 minutes, until the leeks have softened. Season. Add the spinach and cover. Allow the spinach to wilt in the steam for 3–4 minutes, stir into the vegetables and add the pine nuts.

3 Beat the eggs with salt, pepper, the remaining cumin, basil and parsley. Add to the pan and cook over low heat until the bottom of the omelette sets. Pull the edges away from the sides of the pan as it cooks and tilt the pan so that the uncooked egg runs underneath.

4 Preheat the grill (broiler). Flash the frittata under the hot grill to set the egg on top. Cut into wedges and serve warm, garnished with watercress and Parmesan, if you like.

Nutritional information per portion: Energy 227kcal/ 1151kJ; Protein 18g; Carbohydrate 4g, of which sugars 3g; Fat 21g, of which saturates 6g; Cholesterol 330mg; Calcium 277mg; Fibre 4.7g; Sodium 366mg.

Wild mushroom and fontina tart

Use any types of wild mushrooms you like in this tart – chanterelles, morels, horns of plenty and porcini all have wonderful flavours. It makes an impressive vegetarian meal, served with a salad.

SERVES 6

225g/8oz ready-made shortcrust pastry, thawed if frozen
50g/2oz/¼ cup butter
350g/12oz/5 cups mixed wild mushrooms, sliced if large
150g/5oz Fontina cheese, sliced
salt and ground black pepper

1 Preheat the oven to 190°C/375°F/ Gas 5. Roll out the pastry and use to a line a 23cm/9in loose-bottomed flan tin (pan). Chill the pastry for 30 minutes, then bake blind for 15 minutes. Set aside.

2 Heat the butter in a large frying pan until foaming. Add the mushrooms and season with salt and ground black pepper.

3 Cook over medium heat for about 4–5 minutes, moving the mushrooms about and turning them occasionally with a wooden spoon, until golden in colour.

4 Arrange the mushrooms in the cooked pastry case with the Fontina. Return the tart to the oven for 10 minutes, or until the cheese is golden and bubbling. Serve hot.

Nutritional information per portion: Energy 409kcal/1701kJ; Protein 10.2g; Carbohydrate 21.9g, of which sugars 2.3g; Fat 31g, of which saturates 13.4g; Cholesterol 143mg; Calcium 121mg; Fibre 2.3g; Sodium 199mg.

Parmigiana di melanzane

This Italian dish can be served as a vegetarian main course, or as an accompaniment to meat or chicken dishes. For a variation, layer a few artichoke hearts between the slices of aubergine.

SERVES 8

900g/2lb aubergines (eggplant), sliced
    lengthways
60ml/4 tbsp olive oil
600ml/1 pint/2½ cups garlic and herb
    passata (bottled strained tomatoes)
115g/4oz/1¼ cups freshly grated
    Parmesan cheese
salt and ground black pepper

1 Preheat the grill (broiler) to high. Brush the aubergine slices with the oil and season to taste. Arrange them in a single layer on a grill pan and grill (broil) for 4–5 minutes on each side, until golden and tender. (You will have to do this in batches.)

2 Preheat the oven to 190°C/375°F/ Gas 5. Spoon a little passata into a large baking dish.

3 Arrange a single layer of aubergine slices over the top and sprinkle with some grated Parmesan cheese.

4 Repeat the layers of passata, aubergine and Parmesan, finishing with a good sprinkling of Parmesan.

5 Bake for 20–25 minutes, or until golden and bubbling. Serve immediately while hot.

Nutritional information per portion: Energy 172kcal/ 719kJ; Protein 8g; Carbohydrate 8g, of which sugars 8g; Fat 12g, of which saturates 4g; Cholesterol 13mg; Calcium 172mg; Fibre 2.6g; Sodium 250mg.

Rice and aubergine bake

The purple melanzane (aubergine) is used in everything from antipasti to desserts. This recipe is worth all the effort as the finished result looks and tastes spectacular.

SERVES 8

3 large aubergines (eggplants)

2 onions

50g/2oz/1/4 cup unsalted butter

90ml/6 tbsp olive oil, plus extra
    for greasing

30ml/2 tbsp chopped fresh parsley

8 fresh basil leaves, torn into shreds

275g/10oz tomatoes, peeled, seeded
    and cut in quarters

275g/10oz/1 1/2 cups risotto rice

600ml/1 pint/2 1/2 cups hot chicken
    or vegetable stock

45ml/3 tbsp plain (all-purpose) flour

sunflower oil, for shallow frying

115g/4oz/1 cup grated Caciocavallo or Provolone cheese,
    or other semi-hard cheese

sea salt and ground black pepper

1 Trim the aubergines and slice them into rounds 2cm/3/4 inch thick. Spread them out in a colander and sprinkle generously with salt. Stand the colander in the sink, fit a plate inside to cover the aubergines, put a weight on top and leave to drain for 1–2 hours.

2 Meanwhile, peel the onions and put them in a pan. Cover them with water, bring to the boil and cook for 10 minutes. Drain. Allow to cool for about 4–5 minutes, then slice them thinly.

3 Melt the butter with half the olive oil in a pan. Add half the sliced onion and fry for 4–5 minutes until softened. Stir in the parsley and basil. Cook for 5 minutes, then stir in the tomatoes. Season with salt and pepper, cover and simmer for 20 minutes, stirring occasionally.

4 Preheat the oven to 190°C/375°F/Gas 5. Heat the rest of the oil in a flameproof casserole. Add the remaining onion and fry for 4 minutes until transparent. Stir in the rice until shiny and coated in oil, then stir in the stock. Cover the casserole with a lid or foil and put it in the oven. Bake for 15 minutes.

5 Meanwhile, rinse the aubergine slices and pat them dry with kitchen paper. Dust them lightly with flour. Heat the sunflower oil in a frying pan until sizzling. Fry the aubergine slices in batches for 3 minutes on each side or until golden brown. Add more oil to the pan as needed between batches. Lift out the aubergine slices and drain on kitchen paper to remove the excess oil.

6 Take the rice mixture out of the oven and stir in 30–45ml/2–3 tbsp of grated Caciocavallo, Provolone cheese or other semi-hard cheese.

7 Grease a 1.2kg/2½lb round mould with oil, then line the base and sides with aubergine slices. Cover with a layer of the tomato sauce, then with a layer of rice, and then a generous sprinkling of grated Caciocavallo or Provolone. Continue in this way until the mould is full, banging it down firmly on the work surface every now and again to settle the ingredients. Finish with a sprinkling of cheese.

8 Bake for 10 minutes, then remove from the oven and turn out on to a platter. Serve immediately.

Nutritional information per portion: Energy 371kcal/1544kJ; Protein 8.4g; Carbohydrate 38.6g, of which sugars 5.6g; Fat 20.2g, of which saturates 7.8g; Cholesterol 28mg; Calcium 152mg; Fibre 2.9g; Sodium 158mg.

Baked winter squash in tomato sauce

This Italian dish is especially popular in northern Italy, from around Mantua, where the most magnificent squash grows. It is a great accompaniment to meat and chicken main courses.

SERVES 4–6

45–75ml/3–5 tbsp olive oil

1kg/2¹/₂lb pumpkin or orange winter squash, peeled and sliced

1 onion, chopped

3–5 garlic cloves, chopped

2 x 400g/14oz cans chopped tomatoes

pinch of sugar

2–3 sprigs of fresh rosemary, stems removed and leaves chopped

salt and ground black pepper

1 Preheat the oven to 160°C/325°F/ Gas 3. Heat 45ml/3 tbsp of the oil in a pan and fry the pumpkin slices in batches until golden brown, removing them from the pan when cooked.

2 Add the onion to the pan, with more oil if necessary, and fry for 5 minutes until softened. Add the garlic to the pan and cook for 1 minute.

3 Add the tomatoes and sugar to the pan and cook over medium-high heat until slightly thickened. Stir in the rosemary and season to taste.

4 Layer the pumpkin slices and tomato sauce in an ovenproof dish, ending with some sauce. Bake for 35 minutes until the top starts to brown. Serve immediately.

Nutritional information per portion: Energy 94kcal/392kJ; Protein 2.1g; Carbohydrate 7.8g, of which sugars 7g; Fat 6.2g, of which saturates 1.1g; Cholesterol 0mg; Calcium 58mg; Fibre 3g; Sodium 12mg.

Artichokes with **garlic, lemon** and **olive oil**

This classic dish of Florence is not only delicious as a salad, but can also be added to roasted fish, chicken or lamb during cooking to make a tasty casserole.

SERVES 4

4 globe artichokes

juice of 1–2 lemons, plus extra to acidulate water

60ml/4 tbsp extra virgin olive oil

1 onion, chopped

5–8 garlic cloves, roughly chopped or thinly sliced

30ml/2 tbsp chopped fresh parsley

120ml/4fl oz/1/2 cup dry white wine

120ml/4fl oz/1/2 cup vegetable stock or water

salt and ground black pepper

1 Remove the tough outer artichoke leaves. Peel the tender part of the stems and cut into bitesize pieces, then put in a bowl of acidulated water. Cut the artichokes into quarters, cut out the chokes and add the hearts to the bowl.

2 Heat the oil in a pan, add the onion and garlic and fry for 5 minutes until softened. Stir in the parsley and cook for a few seconds. Add the wine, stock, lemon juice and drained artichokes. Season.

3 Bring the mixture to the boil, then lower the heat, cover and simmer for 10–15 minutes until the artichokes are tender. Lift the cooked artichokes out with a slotted spoon and transfer to a serving dish.

4 Bring the cooking liquid to the boil and boil until reduced to about half its volume. Pour the mixture over the artichokes and drizzle over the remaining lemon juice. Taste for seasoning and allow to cool slightly before serving.

Nutritional information per portion: Energy 142kcal/586kJ; Protein 1.6g; Carbohydrate 4.1g, of which sugars 1.9g; Fat 11.3g, of which saturates 1.6g; Cholesterol 0mg; Calcium 40mg; Fibre 1.6g; Sodium 47mg.

Pepper gratin

Serve this simple but delicious dish as a light vegetarian meal with a small mixed leaf or rocket salad and some good crusty bread to mop up the juices from the peppers.

SERVES 4

2 red (bell) peppers
30ml/2 tbsp extra virgin olive oil
60ml/4 tbsp fresh white breadcrumbs
1 garlic clove, finely chopped
5ml/1 tsp drained bottled capers
8 stoned (pitted) black olives,
  roughly chopped
15ml/1 tbsp chopped fresh oregano
15ml/1 tbsp chopped fresh flat
  leaf parsley
salt and ground black pepper
fresh herbs, to garnish

1 Preheat the oven to 200°C/400°F/Gas 6. Place the peppers under a hot grill (broiler). Turn occasionally until they are blackened and blistered all over. Remove from the heat and place in a plastic bag. Seal and leave to cool.

2 When cool, peel the peppers. (Don't skin them under the tap as the water would wash away some of the delicious smoky flavour.) Halve and remove the seeds, then cut the flesh into large strips.

3 Use a little of the olive oil to grease a small ovenproof dish. Arrange the pepper strips in the dish.

4 Sprinkle the remaining ingredients on top, drizzle with the remaining olive oil and add salt and pepper to taste. Bake for about 20 minutes until the breadcrumbs have browned. Garnish with fresh herbs and serve immediately.

Nutritional information per portion: Energy 136kcal/ 567kJ; Protein 2g; Carbohydrate 13g, of which sugars 5g; Fat 9g, of which saturates 1g; Cholesterol 0mg; Calcium 31mg; Fibre 2.4g; Sodium 315mg.

Marinated courgettes

This is a simple vegetable dish that can be eaten hot or cold. It is enjoyed all over Italy, using the best of the season's courgettes. Carrots, onions and green beans are also be prepared this way.

SERVES 4

4 courgettes (zucchini)
60ml/4 tbsp extra virgin olive oil
30ml/2 tbsp chopped fresh mint, plus
   whole leaves, to garnish
30ml/2 tbsp white wine vinegar
salt and ground black pepper
wholemeal Italian bread and green
   olives, to serve

1 Cut the courgettes into thin slices. Heat 30ml/2 tbsp of the oil in a wide frying pan. Fry the courgettes in batches, for 4–6 minutes, until tender and brown around the edges. Transfer the cooked courgettes to a bowl. Season well with salt and black pepper.

2 Heat the remaining oil in the pan, then add the mint and vinegar and let it bubble for a few seconds. Pour the mixture over the courgettes. Leave to marinate for at least 1 hour, then serve, garnished with mint and accompanied by bread and olives.

Nutritional information per portion: Energy 155kcal/ 638kJ; Protein 2g; Carbohydrate 2g, of which sugars 2g; Fat 15g, of which saturates 2g; Cholesterol 0mg; Calcium 14mg; Fibre 2.2g; Sodium 114mg.

Roasted plum tomatoes and garlic

These are so simple to prepare, yet they taste absolutely wonderful. Use a large, shallow earthenware dish that will allow the tomatoes to sear and char in a hot oven.

SERVES 4

8 plum tomatoes, halved
12 garlic cloves
60ml/4 tbsp extra virgin olive oil
3 bay leaves
salt and ground black pepper
45ml/3 tbsp fresh oregano leaves,
    to garnish

1 Preheat the oven to 230°C/450°F/Gas 8. Select an ovenproof dish that will hold all the tomatoes in a single layer. Place the tomatoes in the dish and push the whole, unpeeled garlic cloves between them.

2 Brush the tomatoes with the olive oil, add the bay leaves and sprinkle black pepper over the top.

3 Bake for about 45 minutes until the tomatoes have softened and are sizzling in the pan. They should be charred around the edges.

4 Season with salt and a little more black pepper, if needed. Garnish with fresh oregano leaves and serve.

Nutritional information per portion: Energy 164kcal/ 681kJ; Protein 1g; Carbohydrate 5g, of which sugars 5g; Fat 16g, of which saturates 2g; Cholesterol 0mg; Calcium 14mg; Fibre 2.2g; Sodium 114mg.

Green beans with tomatoes

This is a real summer favourite using the season's best ripe plum tomatoes and green beans. When choosing green beans make sure that they snap easily – this is a good sign of freshness.

SERVES 4

30ml/2 tbsp olive oil

1 large onion, finely sliced

2 garlic cloves, finely chopped

6 large ripe plum tomatoes, peeled, seeded and coarsely chopped

150ml/¼ pint/⅔ cup dry white wine

450g/1 lb green beans, sliced in half lengthways

16 stoned (pitted) black olives

10ml/2 tsp lemon juice

salt and ground black pepper

1 Heat the oil in a large frying pan. Add the onion and garlic and cook for about 5 minutes until the onion is softened but not brown.

2 Add the chopped tomatoes, white wine, beans, olives and lemon juice, and cook over gentle heat for a further 20 minutes, stirring from time to time, until the sauce is thickened and the beans are tender.

3 Season with plenty of salt and pepper to taste and serve immediately.

Nutritional information per portion: Energy 150kcal/ 624kJ; Protein 4g; Carbohydrate 12g, of which sugars 10g; Fat 10g, of which saturates 2g; Cholesterol 0mg; Calcium 72mg; Fibre 6.3g; Sodium 381mg.

Spinach with raisins and pine nuts

Lightly cooked spinach with a little olive oil, onion, raisins and pine nuts is a typical Italian dish, which echoes the sweet-nut combination that is so popular in Greece and Turkey.

SERVES 4

50g/2oz/scant ¹/₂ cup raisins

1kg/2¹/₄lb fresh spinach
  leaves, washed

45ml/3 tbsp olive oil

6–8 spring onions (scallions), thinly
  sliced or 1–2 small yellow or white
  onions, finely chopped

50g/2oz/scant ¹/₂ cup pine nuts

salt and ground black pepper

1 Put the raisins in a small bowl and pour over boiling water to cover. Leave to stand for about 10 minutes until plumped up, then drain.

2 Cook the spinach in a pan over medium-high heat, with only the water that clings to the leaves after washing, for 1–2 minutes until the leaves are bright green and wilted. Remove from the heat and drain well. Leave to cool.

3 When the spinach has cooled, chop with a sharp knife. Heat the oil in a frying pan over medium-low heat, then lower the heat further and add the spring onions or onions.

4 Fry for 5 minutes, or until soft, then add the spinach, raisins and pine nuts. Raise the heat and cook for 2–3 minutes to warm through. Season to taste and serve hot or warm.

Nutritional information per portion: Energy 198kcal/824kJ; Protein 5.2g; Carbohydrate 14.3g, of which sugars 11g; Fat 13.7g, of which saturates 1.6g; Cholesterol 0mg; Calcium 226mg; Fibre 3.1g; Sodium 218mg.

Roasted pepper and tomato salad

This is one of those lovely recipes which brings together perfectly the colours, flavours and textures of southern Italian food. Eat this dish at room temperature with a green salad.

SERVES 4

3 red (bell) peppers
6 large plum tomatoes
2.5ml/$\frac{1}{2}$ tsp dried red chilli flakes
1 red onion, finely sliced
3 garlic cloves, finely chopped
grated rind and juice of 1 lemon
45ml/3 tbsp chopped fresh flat
   leaf parsley
30ml/2 tbsp extra virgin olive oil
salt and ground black pepper
black and green olives and extra
   chopped flat leaf parsley,
   to garnish

1 Preheat the oven to 220°C/425°F/ Gas 7. Place the peppers on a baking sheet and roast, turning occasionally, for 10 minutes or until the skins are almost blackened. Add the tomatoes to the baking sheet and bake for 5 minutes more.

2 Place the peppers in a plastic bag, close the top loosely, trapping in the steam, and then set them aside, with the tomatoes, until they are cool enough to handle.

3 Carefully pull off the skin from the peppers. Remove the seeds, then chop the peppers and tomatoes roughly and place in a mixing bowl.

4 Add the chilli flakes, onion, garlic, lemon rind and juice. Sprinkle over the parsley. Mix well, then transfer to a serving dish. Sprinkle with a little salt, drizzle over the olive oil and sprinkle olives and extra parsley over the top. Serve at room temperature.

Nutritional information per portion: Energy 126kcal/527kJ; Protein 2.9g; Carbohydrate 14.6g, of which sugars 13.8g; Fat 6.6g, of which saturates 1.1g; Cholesterol 0mg; Calcium 49mg; Fibre 4.4g; Sodium 22mg.

Spinach and roast garlic salad

Don't worry about the amount of garlic in this tasty salad. During roasting, the garlic becomes very sweet and subtle and loses its typically pungent taste.

SERVES 4

12 garlic cloves, unpeeled
60ml/4 tbsp extra virgin olive oil
450g/1lb baby spinach leaves
50g/2oz/½ cup pine nuts,
  lightly toasted
juice of ½ lemon
salt and ground black pepper

1 Preheat the oven to 190°C/375°F/Gas 5. Place the garlic in a small roasting pan, toss in 30ml/2 tbsp of the olive oil and bake for about 15 minutes, until the garlic cloves are slightly charred around the edges.

2 While still warm, transfer the garlic to a salad bowl. Add the spinach, pine nuts, lemon juice, remaining olive oil and a little salt. Toss well and add black pepper to taste. Serve immediately.

Nutritional information per portion: Energy 258kcal/ 1065kJ; Protein 6g; Carbohydrate 4g, of which sugars 2g; Fat 25g, of which saturates 3g; Cholesterol 6mg; Calcium 195mg; Fibre 4.4g; Sodium 256mg.

Sweet and sour artichoke salad

Agrodolce is a delicate sweet-and-sour sauce that works perfectly with the combination of flavours from the artichokes, onions and beans in this simple salad.

SERVES 4

6 small globe artichokes
juice of 1 lemon
30ml/2 tbsp olive oil
2 medium onions, roughly chopped
175g/6oz/1 cup fresh or frozen broad
   (fava) beans (shelled weight)
175g/6oz/1½ cups fresh or frozen
   peas (shelled weight)
salt and ground black pepper
fresh mint leaves, to garnish

FOR THE SALSA AGRODOLCE
120ml/4 fl oz/½ cup white wine vinegar
15ml/1 tbsp caster (superfine) sugar
handful of fresh mint leaves, roughly torn

1 Peel the outer leaves from the artichokes and cut into quarters. Place the artichokes in a bowl of water with the lemon juice.

2 Heat the oil in a large pan, add the onions and cook until golden. Add the beans and stir, then drain the artichokes and add to the pan. Pour in 300ml/½ pint/1¼ cups of water and cook, covered, for 10–15 minutes. Add the peas, season and cook for a further 5 minutes, stirring, until the vegetables are tender. Strain and place the vegetables in a bowl, leave to cool, then cover and chill in the refrigerator until required.

3 To make the salsa agrodolce, mix all the ingredients in a small pan. Heat gently for 2–3 minutes until the sugar has dissolved. Simmer gently for about 5 minutes, stirring occasionally. Leave to cool. To serve, drizzle the salsa over the vegetables and garnish with mint leaves.

Nutritional information per portion: Energy 172kcal/717kJ; Protein 8g; Carbohydrate 21g, of which sugars 10.8g; Fat 6.8g, of which saturates 1g; Cholesterol 0mg; Calcium 106mg; Fibre 7.3g; Sodium 82mg.

Ice creams, desserts, bakes and bread

Desserts provide a sweet finale to a meal, and this section includes a collection of delectable hot and cold Italian desserts, as well as delicious cakes, pies and rustic breads. Enjoy delightful desserts such as classic Zabaglione, Tiramisu, and Zucotto, or bakes such as Apple Cake, Chocolate Salami,and Baked Sweet Ravioli, or breads such as Panettone and Focaccia.

Pistachio ice cream

This Italian favourite owes its enduring popularity to its delicate pale green colour and distinctive yet subtle flavour. Buy the pistachio nuts as you need them, as they quickly go stale.

SERVES 6

4 egg yolks
75g/3oz/6 tbsp caster (superfine) sugar
5ml/1 tsp cornflour (cornstarch)
300ml/¹⁄₂ pint/1¹⁄₄ cups semi-skimmed
    (low-fat) milk

115g/4oz/1 cup unsalted pistachios, plus a few extra,
    to decorate
300ml/¹⁄₂ pint/1¹⁄₄ cups whipping cream
a little green food colouring
chocolate-dipped waffle cones,
    to serve (optional)

1 Whisk the egg yolks, sugar and cornflour in a bowl until the mixture is thick and foamy.

2 In a heavy pan, gently bring the milk to the boil, then gradually whisk it into the egg yolk mixture.

3 Return the mixture to the pan and cook it over a gentle heat, stirring constantly until the custard thickens and is smooth. Pour it back into the bowl, set aside to cool, then chill in the refrigerator until required.

4 Shell the pistachios and put them in a food processor or blender. Add 30ml/2 tbsp of the cream and grind the mixture to a coarse paste.

5 Pour the rest of the cream into a small pan. Bring it to the boil, stir in the coarsely ground pistachios, then leave to cool.

6 Mix the chilled custard and pistachio cream together and tint the mixture delicately with a few drops of food colouring.

7 Pour the tinted custard and pistachio mixture into a plastic tub or similar freezerproof container. Freeze for 6 hours, beating once or twice with a fork or an electric whisk to break up the ice crystals.

8 Scoop the ice cream into cones or dishes to serve and sprinkle with a few extra pistachios.

Nutritional information per portion: Energy 422kcal/1749kJ; Protein 8.1g; Carbohydrate 19.1g, of which sugars 17.9g;
Fat 35.3g, of which saturates 15.6g; Cholesterol 190mg; Calcium 133mg; Fibre 1.2g; Sodium 143mg.

Cassata

An irresistible Italian ice cream, cassata *usually comprises three layers, frozen in a bombe mould. This version combines the complementary flavours of pistachio, vanilla and tutti frutti.*

SERVES 6

6 egg yolks
225g/8oz/generous 1 cup caster
   (superfine) sugar
15ml/1 tbsp cornflour (cornstarch)
600ml/1 pint/2¹/₂ cups milk
600ml/1 pint/2¹/₂ cups double (heavy) cream
75g/3oz/³/₄ cup pistachio nuts

2.5ml/¹/₂ tsp almond extract
dash each of green and red food colouring
40g/1¹/₂oz/¹/₄ cup candied peel,
   finely chopped
50g/2oz/¹/₄ cup glacé (candied) cherries,
   washed, dried and finely chopped
5ml/1 tsp vanilla extract

1 Whisk the egg yolks, sugar, cornflour and a little of the milk in a bowl until creamy. Bring the remaining milk and the cream to the boil in a heavy pan.

2 Pour into the egg yolk mixture in a steady stream, whisking well. Pour back into the pan. Cook gently, stirring until thickened, but do not boil. Remove from the heat and divide into three equal quantities. Cover and leave to cool.

3 Cover the pistachio nuts with boiling water in a bowl and leave for 1 minute. Drain and rub between several thicknesses of kitchen paper, to loosen the skins.

4 Roughly chop and add to one bowl with the almond extract and a drop of green food colouring.

5 Stir the candied peel, glacé cherries and a drop of red food colouring into the second bowl. Stir the vanilla extract into the third. Line a dampened 900g/2lb terrine or loaf tin (pan) with baking parchment.

6 Pour the mixtures into 3 separate tubs and freeze until thickened, beating twice. Put the frozen pistachio ice cream into the prepared tin, then the vanilla and the tutti frutti. Freeze overnight.

7 To serve, dip the terrine or tin in very hot water for 2–3 seconds, then place a long serving plate upside down on top of it. Holding together, turn them over. Lift off the container. Peel away the lining paper. Serve in slices.

Nutritional information per portion: Energy 380kcal/1598kJ; Protein 9.3g; Carbohydrate 50.7g, of which sugars 43.8g; Fat 13.3g, of which saturates 7.3g; Cholesterol 97mg; Calcium 72mg; Fibre 1.9g; Sodium 115mg.

Gingered semi-freddo

This Italian ice cream is rather like the original soft-scoop ice cream. Made with a boiled sugar syrup rather than a traditional egg custard, and generously speckled with ginger, this delicious ice cream will stay soft when frozen.

SERVES 6

4 egg yolks
115g/4oz/generous ¹/₂ cup caster
   (superfine) sugar
120ml/4fl oz/¹/₂ cup cold water
300ml/¹/₂ pint/1¹/₄ cups double
   (heavy) cream

115g/4oz/²/₃ cup drained preserved
   stem ginger, finely chopped, plus
   extra slices, to decorate
45ml/3 tbsp whisky (optional)

1 Put the egg yolks in a large heatproof bowl and whisk until frothy. Then, bring a pan of water to the boil and simmer gently.

2 Mix the sugar and measured cold water in another pan and heat gently, stirring occasionally, until the sugar has dissolved.

3 Increase the heat and boil for 4–5 minutes without stirring, until the syrup registers 119°C/238°F on a sugar thermometer. Alternatively, test by dropping a little of the syrup into a cup of cold water. Pour the water away. You should be able to mould the syrup into a ball.

4 Put the bowl of egg yolks over the pan of simmering water and whisk in the sugar syrup. Continue whisking until the mixture is very thick. Remove from the heat and whisk until cool.

5 Whip the cream and lightly fold it into the yolk mixture, with the chopped ginger and whisky, if using. Pour into a plastic tub or similar freezerproof container and freeze for 1 hour.

6 Stir the semi-freddo to bring any ginger that has sunk to the bottom of the tub to the top, then return to the freezer for 5–6 hours until firm. Scoop into dishes or chocolate cases. Decorate with slices of ginger.

Nutritional information per portion: Energy 371kcal/1539kJ; Protein 3g; Carbohydrate 22.4g, of which sugars 22.3g;
Fat 30.6g, of which saturates 17.8g; Cholesterol 203mg; Calcium 55mg; Fibre 0.5g; Sodium 23mg.

Zucotto

A delightful Italian dessert with a rich ricotta, fruit, chocolate and nut filling, zucotto is encased in a moist, chocolate- and liqueur-flavoured sponge.

SERVES 8

3 eggs
75g/3oz/6 tbsp caster (superfine) sugar
75g/3oz/²/₃ cup plain (all-purpose) flour
25g/1oz/¹/₄ cup unsweetened cocoa powder
90ml/6 tbsp Kirsch
250g/9oz/generous 1 cup ricotta cheese
50g/2oz/¹/₂ cup icing (confectioners') sugar
50g/2oz plain (semisweet) chocolate,
    finely chopped

50g/2oz/¹/₂ cup blanched almonds,
    chopped and toasted
75g/3oz/scant ¹/₂ cup natural glacé (candied)
    cherries, quartered
2 pieces preserved stem ginger,
    finely chopped
150ml/¹/₄ pint/²/₃ cup double
    (heavy) cream
unsweetened cocoa powder, for dusting

1 Heat the oven to 180°C/350°F/Gas 4. Grease and line a 23cm/9in cake tin (pan). Whisk the eggs and sugar in a heatproof bowl over a pan of simmering water until thickened. Remove from the heat and whisk for 2 minutes.

2 Fold the flour and cocoa into the bowl with a large metal spoon. Spoon the mixture into the prepared tin and bake for 20 minutes until firm. Leave to cool.

3 Cut the cake horizontally into three layers. Set aside 30ml/2 tbsp of the Kirsch and drizzle the remainder over the layers. Beat the ricotta in a bowl until soft; beat in the icing sugar, chocolate, almonds, cherries, ginger and reserved Kirsch. Pour the cream into a bowl, whip lightly and fold into the ricotta mixture. Chill. Cut a 20cm/8in circle from one sponge layer and set it aside.

4 Cut the remaining sponge cake to fit the bottom of a 2.8 litre/5 pint/12½ cup freezerproof mixing bowl lined with clear film (plastic wrap). Cut more sponge for the sides of the bowl, to cover one third of the way up. Spoon the ricotta filling into the bowl to the height of the sponge, and level. Fit the reserved circle of sponge on top of the filling. Trim off excess sponge around the edges.

5 Cover and freeze overnight. Transfer to the refrigerator 45 minutes before serving to let the filling soften slightly. Invert on to a serving plate and peel away the clear film (plastic wrap). Dust with the cocoa powder and serve in slices.

Nutritional information per portion: Energy 391kcal/1631kJ; Protein 8.7g; Carbohydrate 33.8g, of which sugars 26.1g; Fat 22.7g, of which saturates 11.4g; Cholesterol 111mg; Calcium 66mg; Fibre 1.3g; Sodium 64mg.

Sicilian ricotta cake

The word cassata is often used to describe a layered ice cream cake. In Sicily, however, it is a traditional cake made of layers of succulent sponge, creamy ricotta cheese and mixed peel, steeped in alcohol, and it looks and tastes truly delicious.

SERVES 8–10

675g/1½ lb/3 cups ricotta cheese

finely grated rind of 1 orange

2 sachets of vanilla sugar

75ml/5 tbsp orange-flavoured liqueur

115g/4oz mixed (candied) peel

8 trifle sponge cakes

60ml/4 tbsp freshly squeezed
   orange juice

extra mixed (candied) peel,
   to decorate

1 Push the ricotta cheese through a sieve (strainer) into a large bowl, add the orange rind, vanilla sugar and 15ml/1 tbsp of the liqueur and beat well with a wooden spoon until thoroughly mixed.

2 Transfer about one-third of the mixture to another bowl, cover and chill the mixture until serving time.

3 Finely chop the candied peel and beat into the remaining ricotta cheese mixture until evenly mixed. Set aside while you prepare the loaf tin (pan).

4 Line the base of a 1.2 litre/2 pint/5 cup loaf tin with baking parchment. Cut the trifle sponges in half through their thickness.

5 Arrange four pieces of sponge side by side in the bottom of the loaf tin and sprinkle with 15ml/1 tbsp each of liqueur and orange juice.

6 Put one-third of the ricotta and fruit mixture in the loaf tin and spread the mixture out evenly. Cover with four more pieces of sponge and sprinkle with another 15ml/1 tbsp each of liqueur and orange juice as before.

7 Repeat the alternate layers of ricotta mixture and sponge until all the ingredients are used, soaking the sponge pieces with liqueur and orange juice each time, and ending with soaked sponge. Cover with a piece of baking parchment.

8 Cut a piece of card to fit inside the tin, place on top of the baking parchment and weight down evenly. Chill for 24 hours.

9 To serve, remove the weights, card and paper and run a metal spatula between the sides of the cassata and the tin. Invert a serving plate on top of the cassata, then invert the two so that the cassata is upside down on the plate. Peel off the lining paper.

10 Spread the chilled ricotta mixture over the cassata to cover it completely, then decorate the top with candied peel, cut into fancy shapes. Serve chilled.

Nutritional information per portion: Energy 224kcal/ 936kJ; Protein 7g; Carbohydrate 21g, of which sugars 17g; Fat 6g, of which saturates 3.7g; Cholesterol 52mg; Calcium 189mg; Fibre 0.2g; Sodium 153mg.

Zabaglione

Light as air and wonderfully alcoholic, this warm egg custard is a much-loved Italian pudding. Though traditionally made with Marsala, the fortified wine can be replaced by sweet sherry.

SERVES 4

4 egg yolks
50g/2oz/¹/₄ cup caster (superfine) sugar
60ml/4 tbsp Marsala, Madeira
  or sweet sherry
amaretti, to serve

1 Place the egg yolks and sugar in a large heatproof bowl, and whisk with an electric beater until the mixture is pale and thick.

2 Gradually add the Marsala, Madeira or sherry to the egg mixture, 15ml/1 tbsp at a time, whisking well after each addition.

3 Place the bowl over a pan of gently simmering water and continue to whisk for 5–7 minutes, until the mixture becomes thick; when the beaters are lifted they should leave a thick trail on the surface of the mixture. Do not be tempted to underbeat the mixture, as the zabaglione will be too runny and will be likely to separate.

4 Pour into four warmed, stemmed glasses and serve immediately, with amaretti for dipping.

Nutritional information per portion: Energy 134kcal/561kJ; Protein 3g; Carbohydrate 14.9g, of which sugars 14.9g; Fat 5.5g, of which saturates 1.6g; Cholesterol 202mg; Calcium 31mg; Fibre 0g; Sodium 10mg.

Grilled nectarines and peach syllabub

This dessert is highly addictive, an irresistible syllabub flavoured with peach schnapps. Here, ripe nectarines are used, which look stunning when slightly caramelized on top.

SERVES 8

120ml/4fl oz/¹/₂ cup peach schnapps
juice of ¹/₂ lemon
25g/1oz/¹/₄ cup icing
   (confectioners') sugar
300ml/¹/₂ pint/1¹/₄ cups double
   (heavy) cream
4 large ripe nectarines, halved
   and stoned (pitted)
5ml/1 tsp clear honey
24 amaretti morbidi
   (soft almond macaroons)

1 Mix the peach schnapps, lemon juice and icing sugar in a large, deep bowl. Cover and chill in the refrigerator.

2 Whisking constantly with a hand-held electric whisk, gradually add the cream to the chilled schnapps mixture, until the syllabub just holds its shape. Do not over-whip. Chill the syllabub while you cook the fruit.

3 Brush each of the halved nectarines with a little honey. Place the nectarines on a hot griddle and cook for about 1–2 minutes.

4 Griddle the amaretti morbidi for about 45 seconds on each side, to warm them through and let the surface caramelize a little. Serve the nectarines and amaretti with the syllabub.

Nutritional information per portion: Energy 343kcal/ 1431kJ; Protein 3g; Carbohydrate 26g, of which sugars 25g; Fat 24g, of which saturates 13g; Cholesterol 51mg; Calcium 41mg; Fibre 2.6g; Sodium 18mg.

Apricot panettone pudding

The combination of the light Italian fruit bread, apricots and pecan nuts produces a wonderfully rich version of the traditional bread-and-butter pudding.

SERVES 6

unsalted butter, for greasing
350g/12oz panettone, sliced
   into triangles
25g/1oz/¼ cup pecan nuts
75g/3oz/⅓ cup ready-to-eat dried
   apricots, chopped
500ml/17fl oz/2¼ cups
   semi-skimmed milk
5ml/1 tsp vanilla extract
1 large egg, beaten
30ml/2 tbsp maple syrup
2.5ml/½ tsp grated nutmeg, plus extra
   for sprinkling
demerara sugar, for sprinkling
crème fraîche or double (heavy) cream,
   to serve (optional)

1 Grease a 1 litre/1¾ pint/4 cup baking dish. Arrange half the panettone in the base of the dish, sprinkle over half the pecan nuts and all the dried apricots, then add another layer of panettone on top.

2 Pour the milk into a small pan and add the vanilla extract. Warm the milk over medium heat until it just simmers. In a large bowl, mix together the beaten egg and maple syrup, grate in the nutmeg, then whisk in the hot milk.

3 Preheat the oven to 200°C/400°F/ Gas 6. Pour the milk mixture over the panettone, lightly pressing down each slice so that it is totally submerged in the mixture. Set the dish aside and leave the pudding to stand for at least 10 minutes.

4 Arrange the reserved pecan nuts over the top and sprinkle with the demerara sugar and nutmeg. Bake for about 40 minutes until risen and golden. Serve hot, with a spoonful of créme fraîche if you like.

Nutritional information per portion: Energy 305kcal/ 1282kJ; Protein 10g; Carbohydrate 44g, of which sugars 23g; Fat 11g, of which saturates 3g; Cholesterol 50mg; Calcium 175mg; Fibre 4.5g; Sodium 223mg.

Tiramisu

The name of this classic Italian dessert translates as "pick me up", which is said to derive from the fact that it is so good that it literally makes you swoon when you eat it.

SERVES 4

225g/8oz/1 cup mascarpone

25g/1oz/¼ cup icing (confectioners')
  sugar, sifted

150ml/¼ pint/⅔ cup strong brewed
  coffee, chilled

300ml/½ pint/1¼ cups double
  (heavy) cream

45ml/3 tbsp coffee liqueur such as
  Tia Maria, Kahlúa or Toussaint

115g/4oz Savoiardi (sponge
  finger) biscuits

50g/2oz dark (bittersweet) or
  plain (semisweet) chocolate,
  coarsely grated

unsweetened cocoa powder, for dusting

1 Grease and line a loaf tin (pan) with clear film (plastic wrap). Put the mascarpone and icing sugar in a bowl and beat for 1 minute. Stir in 30ml/2 tbsp of the chilled coffee.

2 Whip the cream with 15ml/1 tbsp of the liqueur until thick, then fold into the mascarpone mixture. Spoon half the mixture into the loaf tin.

3 Mix the remaining coffee and liqueur in a shallow dish.

4 Dip half the biscuits into the coffee mixture, then arrange on top of the mascarpone mixture in a single layer. Spoon the rest of the mascarpone mixture over the biscuits.

5 Dip the remaining biscuits in the coffee mixture, and arrange on top. Drizzle any remaining coffee mixture over the top. Cover and chill for at least 4 hours. Turn the tiramisu out of the loaf tin and sprinkle with grated chocolate and cocoa powder. Serve.

Nutritional information per portion: Energy 215kcl/894kJ; Protein 8.5mg; Carbohydrate 12.4g of which sugars 10.1g; Fat 13.3g of which saturates 5.9g; Cholesterol 118mg; Calcium 22mg; Fibre 0.1g; Sodium 48mg.

Tuscan citrus sponge

This sensational cake comes from the Tuscan town of Pitigliano, where the rich Jewish tradition dates back to the 13th century. Made with matzo and potato flour, it is a delightful kosher treat.

SERVES 6–9

12 eggs, separated
300g/11oz/1½ cups caster
   (superfine) sugar
120ml/4fl oz/½ cup fresh
   orange juice
grated rind of 1 orange
grated rind of 1 lemon
50g/2oz/½ cup potato flour, sifted
90g/3½oz/¾ cup fine matzo meal
   or matzo meal flour, sifted
large pinch of salt
icing (confectioners') sugar,
   for dusting (optional)

1 Preheat the oven to 160°C/325°F/ Gas 3. Whisk the egg yolks in a large bowl until pale and frothy, then whisk in the sugar, orange juice, orange rind and lemon rind.

2 Fold the sifted flours into the egg mixture. In another clean bowl, whisk the egg whites with the salt until stiff, then gently fold into the egg yolk mixture.

3 Pour the cake mixture into a deep, ungreased 25cm/10in cake tin (pan) and bake for about 1 hour, or until a cocktail stick (toothpick), inserted in the centre, comes out clean. Leave to cool in the tin.

4 When cold, turn out the cake and invert it on to a serving plate. Dust the top with a little icing sugar before serving, if you like.

Nutritional information per portion: Energy 328kcal/1381kJ; Protein 11.1g; Carbohydrate 53.7g, of which sugars 40.5g; Fat 8.8g, of which saturates 2.3g; Cholesterol 285mg; Calcium 66mg; Fibre 0.4g; Sodium 109mg.

Apple cake

*This moist cake is best served warm. It comes from Genoa, home of the whisked sponge.
When whipping the cream, add grated lemon rind – it tastes delicious.*

SERVES 6

**675g/1¹/₂lb eating apples, quartered,
    cored, peeled and thinly sliced**
**finely grated rind and juice of
    1 large lemon**
4 eggs
**150g/5oz/³/₄ cup caster
    (superfine) sugar**
**150g/5oz/1¹/₄ cups plain
    (all-purpose) flour**
5ml/1 tsp baking powder
pinch of salt
**115g/4oz/¹/₂ cup butter, melted and
    cooled, plus extra for greasing**
vanilla sugar, for sprinkling
**very finely pared strips of citrus rind,
    to decorate**
whipped cream, to serve

1 Preheat the oven to 180°C/350°F/
Gas 4. Brush a 23cm/9in springform
cake tin (pan) with melted butter
and line the base with baking
parchment. Put the apple slices in a
bowl and pour over the lemon juice.

2 Put the eggs, sugar and lemon rind
in a bowl and whisk until the mixture
is thick and mousse-like.

3 Sift half the flour, all the baking
powder and the salt over the egg
mousse, then fold in gently.

4 Gently fold in the melted butter.
Sift over the remaining flour, fold it
in gently, then add the apples and
fold these in equally gently. Spoon
into the prepared tin and level the
surface. Bake for 40 minutes or until
a skewer comes out clean.

5 Leave to settle in the tin for 10
minutes, then transfer to a wire
rack. Turn the cake the right way up
and sprinkle the vanilla sugar on top.
Decorate with the citrus rind. Serve
warm, with whipped cream.

Nutritional information per portion: Energy 444kcal/ 1864kJ; Protein 8g; Carbohydrate 60g, of which sugars 41g;
Fat 21g, of which saturates 11g; Cholesterol 195mg; Calcium 78mg; Fibre 3.2g; Sodium 323mg.

Italian chocolate ricotta pie

This traditional pie is made with rich dark chocolate, ricotta and sherry and is absolutely glorious. It is best served at room temperature, and travels well so is perfect for picnics.

SERVES 6

225g/8oz/2 cups plain (all-purpose) flour
30ml/2 tbsp unsweetened cocoa powder
60ml/4 tbsp caster (superfine) sugar
115g/4oz/1/2 cup unsalted butter
60ml/4 tbsp dry sherry
whipped cream, to serve

FOR THE FILLING

2 egg yolks
115g/4oz/1/2 cup caster (superfine) sugar
500g/11/4lb/21/2 cups ricotta cheese
finely grated rind of 1 lemon
90ml/6 tbsp dark (bittersweet) chocolate chips
75ml/5 tbsp chopped mixed (candied) peel
45ml/3 tbsp chopped angelica

1 Preheat the oven to 200°C/400°F/Gas 6. Sift the flour and cocoa into a bowl, then stir in the sugar.

2 Rub in the butter until the mixture resembles breadcrumbs, then work in the sherry, using your fingertips, until the mixture binds to a firm dough.

3 Roll out three-quarters of the pastry on a lightly floured surface and line a 24cm/91/2in loose-based flan tin (pan).

4 Make the filling. Beat the egg yolks and sugar in a large bowl, then beat in the ricotta to mix together thoroughly. Stir in the lemon rind, chocolate chips, mixed peel and angelica.

5 Scrape the ricotta mixture into the pastry case and level the surface. Roll out the remaining pastry and cut into strips, then arrange these in a lattice over the pie.

6 Bake for 15 minutes, then lower the oven temperature to 180°C/350°F/Gas 4 and cook for a further 30-35 minutes, until golden brown and firm. Allow to cool in the tin. Cut into slices and serve with a spoonful of whipped cream.

Nutritional information per portion: Energy 498kcal/ 2100kJ; Protein 6g; Carbohydrate 71g, of which sugars 42g; Fat 22g, of which saturates 13g; Cholesterol 112mg; Calcium 88mg; Fibre 1.4g; Sodium 82mg.

Baked sweet ravioli

These delicious sweet ravioli are made with a rich pastry flavoured with lemon, They are then filled with the traditional ingredients used in Sicilian cassata.

SERVES 4

225g/8oz/2 cups plain (all-purpose) flour
65g/2¹/₂oz/¹/₃ cup caster
   (superfine) sugar
90g/3¹/₂oz/¹/₂ cup butter
1 egg
5ml/1 tsp finely grated lemon rind
icing (confectioners') sugar and grated
   chocolate, for sprinkling

FOR THE FILLING

175g/6oz/³/₄ cup ricotta cheese
50g/2oz/¹/₄ cup caster (superfine) sugar
4ml/³/₄ tsp vanilla extract
1 medium egg yolk
15ml/1 tbsp mixed (candied) peel
25 g/1 oz dark (bittersweet) chocolate,
   finely chopped or grated
1 small egg, beaten

1 Put the flour, sugar into a food processor or blender. Add the butter in pieces and process until mixed. Add the egg and lemon rind and continue to mix to a dough. Wrap the dough in clear film (plastic wrap) and chill.

2 To make the filling, strain the ricotta into a bowl. Stir in the sugar, vanilla extract, egg yolk, peel and chocolate until combined. Preheat the oven to 180°C/350°F/Gas 4. Allow the dough to come to room temperature and divide in half. Roll each half between sheets of clear film to make large strips.

3 Place tablespoons of the filling in two rows along one of the dough strips, ensuring there is at least 2.5cm/1in clear space around each spoonful. Brush between the filling with beaten egg. Place the second strip of pastry on top and press down between each mound of filling to seal.

4 Using a 6cm/2¹/₂in pastry (cookie) cutter, cut around each mound to make circular ravioli. Lift each one and press to seal the edges. Place the ravioli on a greased baking sheet and bake for 15 minutes until golden. Serve warm, sprinkled with icing sugar and grated chocolate.

Nutritional information per portion: Energy 631kcal/ 2648kJ; Protein 14g; Carbohydrate 80g, of which sugars 37g; Fat g, of which saturates 17g; Cholesterol 234mg; Calcium 219mg; Fibre 2g; Sodium 234mg.

Lovers' knots

The literal translation of cenci is "rags and tatters", but they are often referred to by the more endearing term of lovers' knots. They are eaten at carnival time in February.

SERVES 4–6

150g/5oz/1¼ cups plain
    (all-purpose) flour
2.5ml/½ tsp baking powder
pinch of salt
30 ml/2 tbsp caster (superfine) sugar,
    plus extra for dusting
1 egg, beaten
about 25ml/1½ tbsp rum
vegetable oil, for deep frying

1 Sift the flour, baking powder and salt into a bowl, then stir in the sugar. Add the egg. Stir with a fork until it is evenly mixed with the flour, then add the rum gradually and mix until the dough draws together. Knead the dough on a lightly floured surface until smooth. Divide into quarters.

2 Roll each piece out to a 15 x 7.5cm/6 x 3in rectangle and trim to make them straight. Cut each rectangle lengthways into six strips, 1cm/½in wide, and tie into a simple knot.

3 Heat the oil in a deep-fat fryer to a temperature of 190°C/375°F/Gas 5, or heat the oil in a deep frying pan (test the temperature of the oil by dropping in a scrap of the dough trimmings – it should turn crisp in about 30 seconds.

4 Deep-fry the knots in batches for 1–2 minutes until crisp and golden. Transfer the cooked knots to kitchen paper with a slotted spoon. Serve warm, dusted with caster sugar.

Nutritional information per portion: Energy 56kcal/236kJ; Protein 0.9g; Carbohydrate 6.2g, of which sugars 1.4g; Fat 3.1g, of which saturates 0.4g; Cholesterol 8mg; Calcium 11mg; Fibre 0.2g; Sodium 3mg.

Spicy fruit cake from Siena

This is a delicious flat cake with a wonderful spicy flavour. Panforte is very rich, so should be cut into small wedges – offer a glass of sparkling wine to go with it.

SERVES 12–14

butter for greasing
175g/6oz/1 cup hazelnuts,
   roughly chopped
75g/3oz/¹⁄₂ cup whole almonds,
   roughly chopped
225g/8oz/1¹⁄₃ cups mixed candied
   fruits, diced
1.5ml/¹⁄₄ tsp ground coriander
4ml/³⁄₄ tsp ground cinnamon
1.5ml/¹⁄₄ tsp ground cloves
1.5ml/¹⁄₄ tsp grated nutmeg
50g/2oz/¹⁄₂ cup plain (all-purpose) flour
115g/4oz/¹⁄₂ cup honey
115g/4oz/generous 1 cup granulated
   (white) sugar
icing (confectioners') sugar, for dusting

1 Preheat the oven to 180°C/350°F/ Gas 4. Grease a 20cm/8in round cake tin (pan) with the butter. Line the base with baking parchment.

2 Spread the nuts on a baking sheet and cook for 10 minutes until lightly toasted. Remove and set aside. Lower the oven temperature to 150°C/300°F/Gas 2.

3 In a bowl, combine the candied fruits, all the spices and the flour and stir together with a wooden spoon. Add the nuts and stir in thoroughly.

4 In a pan, stir together the honey and sugar and bring to the boil. Cook until it reaches 138°C/280°F on a sugar thermometer or when a small bit forms a hard ball when pressed between fingertips in iced water.

5 Immediately pour the sugar syrup into the dry ingredients and stir well. Pour and press into the prepared tin. Bake for 1 hour.

6 Allow to cool completely in the tin and then turn out on to a plate. Dust with icing sugar before serving.

Nutritional information per portion: Energy 196kcal/ 819kJ; Protein 3g; Carbohydrate 22g, of which sugars 19g; Fat 11g, of which saturates 1g; Cholesterol 0mg; Calcium 59mg; Fibre 1.9g; Sodium 47mg.

Chocolate salami

This after-dinner treat resembles a salami in shape, hence its curious name. It is very rich and will serve a lot of people. Slice it very thinly and serve with espresso coffee and amaretto liqueur.

SERVES 8–12

24 Petit Beurre biscuits,
    coarsely crushed
350g/12oz dark (bittersweet) or
    plain (semisweet) chocolate,
    broken into squares
225g/8oz/1 cup unsalted
    butter, softened
60ml/4 tbsp amaretto liqueur
2 egg yolks
50g/2oz/1/2 cup flaked almonds,
    lightly toasted and thinly
    shredded lengthways
25g/1oz/1/4 cup ground almonds

1 Place the chocolate in a large heatproof bowl. Place the bowl over a pan of just simmering water, add a small chunk of the butter and all the liqueur and heat until the chocolate melts, stirring occasionally.

2 Remove the bowl from the heat, allow to cool then stir in the egg yolks then the remaining butter, a little at a time.

3 Add most of the crushed biscuits, leaving behind a handful, and mix. Stir in the shredded almonds. Leave the mixture in a cold place to stiffen.

4 Process the remaining crushed biscuits in a food processor or blender until very fine. Transfer to a bowl and mix with the ground almonds. Cover and set aside.

5 Turn the mixture on to a sheet of oiled baking parchment, then shape into a 35cm/14in sausage. Wrap and freeze for at least 4 hours until solid.

6 To serve, unwrap the salami. Spread the ground biscuits and almonds out and roll the salami until evenly coated. Leave to stand for about 1 hour. Serve in slices.

Nutritional information per portion: Energy 453kcal/1885kJ; Protein 4.5g; Carbohydrate 36.6g, of which sugars 26.9g; Fat 32.3g, of which saturates 16.8g; Cholesterol 96mg; Calcium 47mg; Fibre 1.4g; Sodium 173mg.

Italian glazed lemon rings

These delicate and pretty cookies look almost too good to eat. The icing is flavoured with a delectable Italian liqueur, Limoncello, so they are strictly a treat for adults.

MAKES ABOUT 16

200g/7oz/1¾ cups self-raising
   (self-rising) flour
50g/2oz/¼ cup unsalted butter, at room
   temperature, diced
25ml/1½ tbsp milk
50g/2oz/¼ cup caster (superfine) sugar
finely grated rind of ½ lemon
1 egg, beaten

FOR THE TOPPING

150g/5oz/1¼ cups icing (confectioners')
   sugar, sifted
30ml/2 tbsp Limoncello liqueur
15ml/1 tbsp chopped candied angelica

1 Preheat the oven to 180°C/350°F/ Gas 4. Line two large baking sheets with baking parchment. Put the flour into a bowl and rub in the butter.

2 Put the milk, sugar and lemon rind in a small pan and stir over a low heat until the sugar has dissolved. Add to the flour mixture, together with the egg, and mix well. Knead lightly until smooth.

3 Roll walnut-size pieces of dough into strands 15cm/6in long. Twist two strands together, and join the ends to make a circle. Place on the prepared baking sheets and bake for 15–20 minutes, or until golden.

4 To make the topping, stir the icing sugar and liqueur together. Dip the top of each cookie into the topping and sprinkle with angelica.

Nutritional information per portion: Energy 125kcal/530kJ; Protein 1.7g; Carbohydrate 23.5g, of which sugars 14g; Fat 3.1g, of which saturates 1.8g; Cholesterol 19mg; Calcium 28mg; Fibre 0.4g; Sodium 25mg.

Chocolate Florentines

These big, flat, crunchy cookies are just like traditional florentines but use tiny seeds instead of nuts. Rolling the edges in milk or white chocolate makes them feel like a real treat.

MAKES 12

50g/2oz/¼ cup unsalted butter
50g/2oz/¼ cup caster (superfine) sugar
15ml/1 tbsp milk
25g/1oz/scant ¼ cup pumpkin seeds
40g/1½oz/generous ¼ cup
   sunflower seeds
50g/2oz/scant ½ cup raisins
25g/1oz/2 tbsp multi-coloured glacé
   (candied) cherries, chopped
30ml/2 tbsp plain (all-purpose) flour
125g/4¼oz milk or white chocolate

1 Preheat the oven to 180°C/350°F/ Gas 4. Line two baking sheets with baking parchment and grease well.

2 In a pan, melt the butter with the sugar, stirring, until the sugar has dissolved, then cook until bubbling. Remove the pan from the heat and stir in the milk, pumpkin and sunflower seeds, raisins, glacé cherries and flour. Mix well.

3 Spoon 6 teaspoonfuls of the mixture on to each baking sheet, spacing them well apart. Bake for 8–10 minutes until golden. Leave for 5 minutes to firm up, then transfer to a wire rack to cool.

4 Melt the chocolate. Roll the edges of the cookies in the chocolate and leave to set on a clean sheet of baking parchment for about 1 hour.

Nutritional information per portion: Energy 157kcal/656kJ; Protein 2.2g; Carbohydrate 17.5g, of which sugars 14.8g; Fat 9.1g, of which saturates 4.3g; Cholesterol 11mg; Calcium 40mg; Fibre 0.6g; Sodium 38mg.

Orange biscotti

These crunchy cookies are based on a traditional Italian recipe in which the cookies are packed with nuts and baked twice. This version is flavoured with orange instead of the nuts.

MAKES ABOUT 20

50g/2oz/¼ cup unsalted butter, at room temperature, diced
90g/3½oz/½ cup light muscovado (brown) sugar
1 egg
finely grated rind of 1 small orange, plus 10ml/2 tsp juice
175g/6oz/1½ cups self-raising (self-rising) flour
7.5ml/1½ tsp baking powder
good pinch of ground cinnamon
50g/2oz/½ cup polenta
icing (confectioners') sugar, for dusting

1 Preheat the oven to 160°C/325°F/Gas 3. Grease a large baking sheet. In a bowl, beat together the butter and sugar until smooth. Beat in the egg, then the orange rind and juice, flour, baking powder, cinnamon and polenta.

2 Transfer the mixture to a lightly floured surface and knead. Place the dough on the baking sheet and flatten out with the palm of your hand to make a rectangle about 25 x 18cm/10 x 7in.

3 Bake the dough for 25 minutes, then remove from the oven and leave to stand for about 5 minutes until slightly cooled. Using a sharp knife, carefully cut the mixture widthways into thin sticks.

4 Space the cookies out slightly on the baking sheet so there is a gap in between each one allowing air to circulate, then return to the oven and bake for a further 20 minutes until crisp. Transfer the biscotti to a wire rack and leave to cool. Serve, dusted with a little icing sugar.

Nutritional information per portion: Energy 80kcal/337kJ; Protein 1.4g; Carbohydrate 13.6g, of which sugars 5.1g; Fat 2.5g, of which saturates 1.4g; Cholesterol 15mg; Calcium 17mg; Fibre 0.3g; Sodium 19mg.

Coffee biscotti

These crisp Italian biscuits are made twice as delicious by adding both freshly roasted ground coffee beans and strong aromatic brewed coffee to the mixture.

MAKES ABOUT 30

25g/1oz/⅓ cup espresso-roasted
  coffee beans
115g/4oz/⅔ cup blanched almonds
200g/7oz/scant 2 cups plain
  (all-purpose) flour
7.5ml/1½ tsp baking powder
1.5ml/¼ tsp salt
75g/3oz/6 tbsp unsalted
  butter, cubed
150g/5oz/¾ cup caster
  (superfine) sugar
2 eggs, beaten
25–30ml/1½–2 tbsp strong
  brewed coffee
5ml/1 tsp ground cinnamon,
  for dusting

1 Preheat the oven to 180°C/350°F/Gas 4. Put the espresso coffee beans in a single layer on one side of a large baking sheet and the almonds on the other. Roast in the oven for 10 minutes. Leave to cool.

2 Put the coffee beans in a blender or food processor and process until fairly fine. Pour out and set aside. Process the almonds until finely ground.

3 Sift the flour, baking powder and salt into a bowl. Rub in the butter until the mixture resembles fine breadcrumbs. Stir in the caster sugar, ground coffee and almonds. Add the beaten eggs and enough brewed coffee to make a fairly firm dough. Lightly knead for a few seconds until smooth and shape into two rolls about 7.5cm/3in in diameter. Place on a greased baking sheet and dust with cinnamon. Bake for 20 minutes.

4 Cut the rolls into 4cm/1½in slices on the diagonal. Arrange them on the baking sheet and bake for 10 minutes, until lightly browned. Cool on a rack.

Nutritional information per portion: Energy 97kcal/409kJ; Protein 2g; Carbohydrate 12.9g, of which sugars 5.7g; Fat 4.4g, of which saturates 1.4g; Cholesterol 12mg; Calcium 37mg; Fibre 0.6g; Sodium 54mg.

Candied fruit and nut roll

This is a traditional cake of Trieste, in the far north-east of Italy. A spiral-shaped bread is filled with nuts and candied fruit, scented with grappa and enriched with butter, eggs and sugar. It is wonderful with milky coffee or hot chocolate, or at the end of a meal with a glass of chilled wine.

SERVES 8

30g/1¹/₄oz fresh yeast

675g/1¹/₂lb/6 cups plain (all-purpose) flour, plus extra for dusting

5 eggs

150g/5oz/²/₃ cup sugar

150g/5oz/10 tbsp unsalted butter, softened, plus extra for greasing

30ml/2 tbsp grappa

grated rind of 1 lemon

90–105ml/6–7 tbsp milk

75g/3oz/¹/₂ cup sultanas (golden raisins)

60ml/4 tbsp dessert wine

75ml/5 tbsp unblanched almonds

90ml/6 tbsp shelled walnuts

40g/1¹/₂oz/¹/₄ cup mixed (candied) peel

40g/1¹/₂oz/¹/₄ cup candied orange peel

30ml/2 tbsp pine nuts

grated rind of 1 orange

15ml/1 tbsp dried fine breadcrumbs

sea salt

1 Put the yeast in a bowl and mix in 75–90ml/5–6 tbsp tepid water. Stir in 115g/4oz/1 cup flour, then leave to stand for about 20 minutes.

2 Beat 3 eggs. Put them into a large bowl with the remaining flour, 115g/4oz/generous ¹/₂ cup sugar, 115g/4oz/¹/₂ cup butter, 15ml/1 tbsp grappa, a pinch of salt and the lemon rind.

3 Add the yeast and flour mixture and knead everything together. Remove the dough from the bowl and knead to form a soft dough, adding the milk to the mixture, a little at a time. You may not need to add all the milk.

4 Put the dough back into the bowl, cover with a dampened dish towel and leave to rise in a warm place for 2 hours, or until doubled in size. Meanwhile, put the sultanas into a small bowl and pour over the dessert wine to cover. Leave the sultanas to swell.

5 Put the almonds and walnuts into a small bowl and pour over enough boiling water to cover. Leave to stand for 2–3 minutes, then peel off the skins. Chop the blanched nuts and the candied peels, then put them into a bowl with the pine nuts, grated orange rind, the drained sultanas and the remaining grappa. Mix well.

6 Heat 15g/¹/₂oz/1 tbsp butter in a frying pan, add the breadcrumbs and fry until crispy. Add to the fruit mixture.

7 Preheat the oven to 190°C/375°F/Gas 5, and grease and flour a baking sheet. Separate 1 egg. Beat the egg yolk and set aside. Put the egg white into a clean, grease-free bowl and whisk until stiff. Mix the remaining egg into the fruit mixture, then fold in the egg white.

8 Knock back (punch down) the dough on a floured surface and roll out to 2cm/^{3}/$_4$in thick. Spread the filling over the dough, then roll it up to make a spiral.

9 Transfer to the baking sheet and brush with the beaten egg yolk. Sprinkle with the remaining sugar and dot with the remaining butter. Bake for about 45 minutes, or until golden brown and cooked through.

Nutritional information per portion: Energy 787kcal/3306kJ; Protein 19.2g; Carbohydrate 102.9g, of which sugars 35.3g; Fat 34.7g, of which saturates 12.8g; Cholesterol 210mg; Calcium 240mg; Fibre 4.8g; Sodium 274mg.

Panettone

This classic Italian bread can be found throughout Italy around Christmas. It is a surprisingly light bread even though it is rich with butter and dried fruit.

MAKES 1 LOAF

400g/14oz/3¹/₂ cups strong white
   bread flour
2.5ml/¹/₂ tsp salt
15g/¹/₂ oz fresh yeast
120ml/4fl oz/¹/₂ cup lukewarm milk
2 eggs
2 egg yolks

75g/3oz/6 tbsp caster (superfine) sugar
150g/5oz/²/₃ cup butter, softened
115g/4oz/²/₃ cup mixed chopped
   (candied) peel
75g/3oz/¹/₂ cup raisins
melted butter, for brushing

1 Using a double layer of baking parchment, line and butter a 15cm/6in deep cake tin (pan) or soufflé dish. Finish the paper 7.5cm/3in above the top of the tin.

2 Sift the flour and salt together into a large bowl. Make a well in the centre. Cream the yeast with 60ml/4 tbsp of the milk, then mix in the remainder. Pour the yeast mixture into the centre of the flour, add the whole eggs and mix in sufficient flour to make a thick batter. Sprinkle a little of the remaining flour over the top and leave in a warm place, for 30 minutes.

3 Add the egg yolks and sugar and mix to a soft dough. Work in the softened butter, then turn out on to a lightly floured surface and knead for 5 minutes until smooth and elastic. Place in a lightly oiled bowl, cover with lightly oiled clear film (plastic wrap) and leave to rise, in a slightly warm place, for 1¹/₂–2 hours, or until doubled in bulk.

4 Knock back (punch down) the dough and turn out on to a lightly floured surface. Gently knead in the peel and raisins. Shape into a ball and place in the prepared tin. Cover with lightly oiled clear film and leave to rise, in a slightly warm place, for about 1 hour, or until doubled.

5 Meanwhile, preheat the oven to 190°C/375°F/Gas 5. Brush the surface with melted butter and cut a cross in the top using a sharp knife. Bake for 20 minutes, then reduce the oven temperature to 180°C/350°F/Gas 4. Brush the top with butter again and bake for a further 25–30 minutes, or until golden. Cool in the tin for 5–10 minutes, then turn out on to a wire rack to cool.

Nutritional information per portion: Energy 2453kcal/10412kJ; Protein 62.2g; Carbohydrate 515.1g, of which sugars 210.3g; Fat 30.7g, of which saturates 8.2g; Cholesterol 791mg; Calcium 1032mg; Fibre 19.4g; Sodium 1590mg.

Olive bread

Black and green olives and good-quality, fruity olive oil combine to make this strongly flavoured and irresistible Italian bread. It is a basic recipe, but tastes really good.

MAKES 1 LOAF

275g/10oz/2¹/₂ cups strong white
    bread flour

50g/2oz/¹/₂ cup strong wholemeal
    (whole-wheat) bread flour

6g/¹/₄ oz sachet easy-blend
    (rapid-rise) dried yeast

2.5ml/¹/₂ tsp salt

210ml/7¹/₂ fl oz/scant 1 cup
    lukewarm water

15ml/1 tbsp extra virgin olive oil,
    plus extra, for brushing

115g/4oz/1 cup pitted (stoned)
    black and green olives,
    coarsely chopped

1 Lightly grease a baking sheet. Mix the flours, yeast and salt together in a large bowl and make a well in the centre. Add the water and oil to the centre of the flour and mix to a soft dough.

2 Knead the dough on a lightly floured surface for 8–10 minutes until smooth and elastic. Place in a lightly oiled bowl, cover with lightly oiled clear film (plastic wrap) and leave in a warm place, for 1 hour, or until doubled in bulk.

3 Turn out on to a lightly floured surface and knock back (punch down). Flatten out and sprinkle over the olives. Fold up and knead. Leave to rest for 5 minutes, then shape into an oval loaf. Place on the prepared baking sheet.

4 Make 6 deep cuts in the top of the loaf, and gently push the sections over. Cover with lightly oiled clear film and leave to rise, in a warm place, for 30–45 minutes, or until doubled in size.

5 Meanwhile, preheat the oven to 200°C/400°F/Gas 6. Brush the bread with olive oil and bake for 35 minutes. Transfer to a wire rack to cool.

Nutritional information per portion: Energy 1325kcal/5600kJ; Protein 31.6g; Carbohydrate 252.5g, of which sugars 4.9g; Fat 27.8g, of which saturates 4.2g; Cholesterol 0mg; Calcium 525mg; Fibre 13.4g; Sodium 3557mg.

Italian chocolate bread

Pane al cioccolato is a slightly sweet chocolate bread from Italy that is often served with creamy mascarpone cheese as a dessert or snack. The dark chocolate pieces add texture to this light loaf.

MAKES 1 LOAF

350g/12oz/3 cups strong white
   bread flour
25ml/1¹/₂ tbsp unsweetened
   cocoa powder
2.5ml/¹/₂ tsp salt
25g/1oz/2 tbsp caster (superfine) sugar
15g/¹/₂ oz fresh yeast
250ml/8fl oz/1 cup lukewarm water
25g/1oz/2 tbsp butter, softened
75g/3oz plain (semisweet) chocolate,
   coarsely chopped
melted butter, for brushing

1 Grease a 15cm/6in round deep cake tin (pan). Sift the flour, cocoa powder and salt together into a bowl. Stir in the sugar. Make a well in the centre.

2 Cream the yeast with 60ml/4 tbsp of the water, then stir in the rest. Add to the centre of the flour mixture and gradually mix to a dough. Knead in the softened butter, then knead on a floured surface until smooth and elastic. Place in a lightly oiled bowl, cover with lightly oiled clear film (plastic wrap) and leave to rise, in a warm place, for about 1 hour, or until doubled in bulk.

3 Turn out on to a lightly floured surface and knock back (punch down). Gently knead in the chocolate, then cover with lightly oiled clear film; leave to rest for 5 minutes. Shape the dough into a round and place in the tin. Cover with lightly oiled clear film and leave to rise, in a warm place, for 45 minutes, or until doubled; the dough should reach the top of the tin.

4 Preheat the oven to 220°C/425°F/Gas 7. Bake for 10 minutes, then reduce the oven temperature to 190°C/375°F/Gas 5 and bake for a further 25–30 minutes. Brush the top with melted butter and leave to cool on a wire rack.

Nutritional information per portion: Energy 1939kcal/ 8188kJ; Protein 41g; Carbohydrate 349g, of which sugars 79g; Fat 52g, of which saturates 30g; Cholesterol 58mg; Calcium 555mg; Fibre 12.6g; Sodium 1388mg.

Focaccia

This dimple-topped Italian flat bread is punctuated with olive oil and the aromatic flavours of sage and garlic to produce a truly succulent loaf that is perfect for all occasions.

MAKES 2 ROUND LOAVES

20g/³⁄₄ oz fresh yeast
325–350ml/11–12fl oz/1¹⁄₃–1¹⁄₂ cups
    lukewarm water
45ml/3 tbsp extra virgin olive oil
500g/1¹⁄₄ lb/5 cups white bread flour
10ml/2 tsp salt
15ml/1 tbsp chopped fresh sage

FOR THE TOPPING

60ml/4 tbsp extra virgin olive oil
4 garlic cloves, chopped
12 fresh sage leaves

1 Lightly oil 2 shallow round cake tins (pan) or pizza pans. Cream the yeast with 60ml/4 tbsp of the water, then stir in the remaining water. Stir in the oil.

2 Sift the flour and salt together into a bowl and make a well in the centre. Pour the yeast mixture into the well and mix to a soft dough.

3 Turn out the dough on to a lightly floured surface and knead for about 8–10 minutes until smooth and elastic. Place in a lightly oiled bowl, cover with lightly oiled clear film (plastic wrap), and leave to rise, in a warm place, for about 1–1¹⁄₂ hours, or until the dough has doubled in bulk.

4 Knock back (punch down) the dough and turn out on to a lightly floured surface. Gently knead in the chopped sage. Divide the dough into 2 equal pieces. Shape each into a ball, roll out into 25cm/10in circles and place in the prepared tins.

5 Cover with lightly oiled clear film and leave to rise in a warm place for about 30 minutes. Uncover, and, using your fingertips, poke the dough to make deep dimples over the entire surface. Replace the clear film cover and leave to rise until doubled in bulk.

6 Meanwhile, preheat the oven to 200°C/400°F/Gas 6. Drizzle over the olive oil for the topping and sprinkle each focaccia evenly with chopped garlic. Dot the sage leaves over the surface. Bake for 25–30 minutes, or until both loaves are golden. Immediately remove the focaccia from the tins and transfer them to a wire rack to cool slightly. These loaves are best served warm.

Nutritional information per portion: Energy 1661kcal/7020kJ; Protein 37.6g; Carbohydrate 310.8g, of which sugars 6g; Fat 38.2g, of which saturates 5.5g; Cholesterol 0mg; Calcium 561mg; Fibre 12.4g; Sodium 3942mg.

The Italian kitchen

The key to Italian cooking is high-

quality basic ingredients. Most Italian

dishes are actually very simple and

focus on just a few fundamental

elements, so it is vital that these

should be as fresh as possible.

This useful guide provides information

on the huge range of Italian produce

and shows you to to prepare and

cook with it.

Pasta

This is the one ingredient that probably sums up the essence of Italian cooking, and it is an essential part of many Italian meals. It is a wonderfully simple and nutritious food which is available in a wealth of shapes and sizes. There are two basic types of pasta, fresh and dried.

Fresh pasta

Home-made fresh pasta is usually made by hand using superfine plain (all-purpose) white flour enriched with eggs. It is often wrapped around a stuffing of meat, fish, vegetables or cheese to make filled pasta such as ravioli or tortellini, or layered with meat or vegetable sauces to make a tasty lasagne. Commercially produced fresh pasta is made with durum wheat, water and eggs. The flavour and texture of all fresh pasta is very delicate, so it is best suited to slightly more creamy sauces.

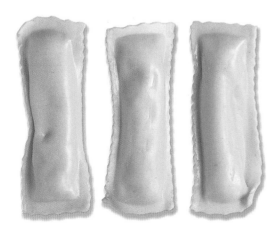

ABOVE: *Fresh filled cannelloni*

ABOVE: *Dried orecchiette*

Dried pasta

This is produced from a dough made from hard durum wheat. It is then shaped into numerous different forms, from long, thin spaghetti to elaborate spirals and frilly bow shapes. Dried pasta can be made from basic pasta dough, which consists of durum wheat and water, or it can be made from a dough enriched with eggs, or coloured and flavoured with ingredients such as spinach, herbs, tomatoes or squid ink. Dried pasta has a nutty flavour and should always retain a firm texture when cooked. It is generally used in preference to fresh pasta for thinner-textured, more robust sauces.

Buying and storing pasta

Choose dried pasta that is made from Italian durum wheat and store it in a cool, dry place. Once opened, dried pasta will keep for weeks in an airtight container. Home-made fresh pasta will only keep for a couple of days, but it also freezes very well.

Commercially made fresh pasta (fresh pasta that is available in a chilled compartment in the supermarket) is pasteurized and vacuum-packed, so it will keep in the fridge for about two weeks, or it can be frozen for up to six months. When buying coloured and flavoured pasta, make sure that it has been made with natural ingredients.

Pasta varieties

Typical pasta shapes can be divided roughly into four categories: short, long strands or ribbons, flat, and filled.

Short pasta

Short pasta covers a wide variety of shapes, the more common types being macaroni, rigati, rigatoni and tubetti. Pasta shapes vary and the list is almost endless, with some wonderfully descriptive names. There are cappellacci (little hats), orecchiette (little ears) or maltagliati (badly cut), penne (quills), conchiglie (little shells), farfalle (bows) and lumache (snails).

ABOVE: *Plain and spinach farfalle*

ABOVE: *Fresh tomato, spinach and plain tagliatelle*

Long or ribbon pasta

The best-known long variety is spaghetti, which also comes in a thinner version, spaghettini, and the flatter linguine, which means "little tongues". Bucatini are thicker and hollow – perfect for trapping sauces in the cavity. Ribbon pasta is wider than the strands and fettucine, tagliatelle and trenette all fall into this category. Dried tagliatelle is usually sold folded into nests, which unravel during cooking. Pappardelle are the widest ribbon pasta; they are often served with a rabbit sauce. The thinnest pasta strands are vermicelli (little worms) and ultra-fine capelli d'angelo (angel's hair).

Flat pasta

In Italy, fresh flat pasta is often called maccheroni, not to be confused with the short tubes of macaroni with which we are familiar. Lasagne and cannelloni are larger flat rectangles of pasta, used for layering or rolling round a filling; dried cannelloni are already formed into wide tubes. Layered pasta dishes like this are cooked in the oven.

Filled pasta

Dried and fresh filled pastas are available in many varieties, and there are dozens of names for filled pasta, but the only difference lies in the shape and size. Ravioli are square, tortelli and agnolotti are usually round, while tortellini and anellini are ring-shaped.

Gnocchi

These can be made from semolina (milled durum wheat), flour, potatoes or ricotta and spinach, and may be shaped like elongated shells, ovals, cylinders or flat discs, or roughly shredded into strozzapreti (priest stranglers). Gnocchi can be served like any pasta.

ABOVE: *Gnocchi*

Pasta with eggs

The best place to make, knead and roll out pasta dough is on a wooden kitchen table.

1 Mound 300g/11oz/2¾ cups plain (all-purpose) flour on a clean surface and make a deep well in the centre.

2 Crack 3 eggs into the well, then add 5ml/1 tsp salt. With a knife or fork, mix the eggs and salt together, then gradually start incorporating the flour from the sides of the well.

3 As soon as the egg mixture is no longer liquid, use your fingers to work the ingredients together until they form a rough and sticky dough. Scrape up any dough that sticks to the work surface with a knife, then scrape this off the knife with your fingers. If the dough is too dry, add a few drops of cold water; if it is too moist, sprinkle a little flour over it.

4 Press the dough into a rough ball and knead it. Push it away from you with the heel of your hand, then fold the end of the dough back on itself so that it faces towards you and push it out again.

5 The dough should be very smooth and elastic. Wrap the dough in clear film (plastic wrap) and leave to rest for 15–20 minutes at room temperature. It will then be ready to roll out.

• To make a chilli-flavoured dough, add 5–10ml/1–2 tsp crushed dried red chilli to the eggs in the well.

Rice, grains and pulses

Almost as important as pasta in Italian cooking are rice, polenta and pulses, which all appear as primi piatti (first courses) in various guises. Like all agricultural countries, Italy relied heavily on protein-rich ingredients when luxuries like meat were in short supply, and a host of wholesome and delicious recipes were developed using these modest ingredients.

ABOVE: *Farro*

Rice (riso)

Italy produces more rice and a greater variety of rice than anywhere else in Europe. Most of it is grown in the Po Valley in Piedmont, where conditions are perfect for cultivating the short-grain Carnaroli, Arborio and Vialone Nano rice, which make the best

BELOW: *Superfino Carnaroli rice is one of the finest Italian rices. Its ability to absorb liquid and cook to a creamy smoothness while still retaining its shape makes it perfect for risotto.*

risotto. Italian rice is classified by size, ranging from the shortest, roundest ordinario (used for puddings) to semifino (for soups and salads), then fino and finally the longer grains of the finest risotto rice, superfino. Superfino rice swells to at least three times its original size during cooking, enabling it to absorb all the cooking liquid while still retaining its shape and firm al dente texture, combined with a creamy smoothness.

Rice is often used in Italian soups; it combines well with almost all vegetables and makes a substantial addition to minestrone. Baked rice dishes are also popular. Cooked rice is layered in a buttered ovenproof dish with meatballs, vegetables or poultry and cheese, then topped with breadcrumbs and baked in the oven. The Italians never serve main dishes on a bed of rice, but prefer to serve plain boiled rice on its own with plenty of butter and cheese stirred in.

Farro

This is the Tuscan name for spelt, a hard brown wheat with pointed grains, which is little used in other parts of Italy. Farro is much harder than other wheat and therefore takes longer to process and cook, but it will grow even in poor soil. In Tuscany it is used to make gran farro, a delicious and nourishing soup, which is served as a first course instead of pasta.

Polenta

For centuries, polenta has been a staple food of the north of Italy, particularly around Friuli and the Veneto. This grainy yellow flour is a type of cornmeal made from ground maize, which is cooked into a kind of porridge with a wide variety of uses. Polenta is sometimes branded according to the type of maize from which it is made. Granturco and Fioretto are the most common types.

In Italy, polenta is available ground to various degrees of coarseness to suit different dishes, but there are two

ABOVE: *Fine polenta*

ABOVE: *Chickpeas*

ABOVE: *Canned broad beans*

ABOVE: *Canned borlotti beans*

main types – coarse and fine. Coarse polenta has a more interesting texture but takes longer to cook.

It is possible to buy quick-cooking polenta, which can be prepared in only 5 minutes. However, if you can spare the 20 minutes or so that it takes to cook traditional polenta, it is best to buy this for its superior texture and flavour. Whether you choose coarse or fine cornmeal is a matter of personal preference; for soft polenta or sweet dishes, fine-ground is better, while course-ground meal is better for frying. Once you have opened the bag, put the remaining polenta in an airtight container; it will keep for at least a month.

Broad beans (fave)
Broad (fava) beans are best eaten fresh from the fat green pod in late spring and early summer, when they are very small and tender with a bittersweet flavour. They are popular in the area around Rome, where they are eaten raw with prosciutto crudo, salami or Pecorino. Later in the season, they should be cooked and skinned (hold the hot beans under cold running water; the skin will slip

off quite easily). Cooked beans have a milder flavour than raw and are excellent with ham and pancetta. Dried beans should be soaked, and the skins removed before cooking. They are used for soups and stews and need about 45 minutes cooking.

Chickpeas (ceci)
These round golden pulses have a distinctive, nutty flavour. They are the oldest of all known pulses and have become very popular in Italian country cooking.

Chickpeas are cooked and used in the same way as haricot (navy) beans. They can be served cold, dressed with lemon juice, chopped fresh herbs and olive oil, to make a substantial salad.

Haricot beans (fagioli)
The most popular varieties of haricot (navy) beans include the pretty red-and-cream speckled borlotti, the small white cannellini (a kind of kidney bean), the larger toscanelli and fagioli coll'occhio (black-eyed beans). All these are eaten as hearty stews, with pasta and in soups, and cannellini are often served simply as a side dish with extra virgin olive oil.

Haricot beans can be made into any number of nutritious soups and stews, or served as the basis of a substantial salad like tonno e fagioli (tuna and beans).

Recipe for basic polenta
To make a basic polenta for 4–6 people, bring to the boil 1.5 litres/2$\frac{1}{2}$ pints/6 cups salted water or stock.

Gradually add 300g/11oz/2 cups polenta in a steady stream, stirring continuously with a wooden spoon. Continue cooking, stirring all the time, until the polenta comes away from the sides of the pan. This will take 20–30 minutes (5 minutes for quick-cooking polenta).

Cheeses

Italy has a great variety of cheeses, ranging from fresh, mild creations like mozzarella to aged, hard cheeses with a very mature flavour, such as Parmesan. All types of milk are used, including ewe's, goat's and buffalo's, which produces the best mozzarella, and some cheeses are made from a mixture of milks.

HARD CHEESES
Parmesan
This is by far the best-known of the Italian hard cheeses. There are two basic types – Parmigiano Reggiano and Grana Padano – but the former is infinitely superior.

Parmigiano-Reggiano
This hard cheese can be made only in a strictly defined zone, which lies between Parma, Modena, Reggio-Emilia, Bologna and Mantua. It takes about 600 litres/132 gallons of milk to make one 30–35kg/ 70–80lb wheel of Parmigiano-Reggiano. The milk is partially skimmed and some of the whey from the previous day's cheese-making is added, then the mixture is carefully heated before rennet is added to encourage curdling. (The rest of the whey is fed to local pigs destined to become prosciutto.) The curds are poured into wheel-shaped forms and the cheese is aged for a minimum of two years; a really fine Parmesan may be aged for up to seven years. During this time, it is nurtured like fine wine, until it becomes pale golden with a slightly granular flaky texture and a nutty, mildly salty flavour. Authentic Parmigiano-Reggiano has the word "Reggiano" stamped on the rind.

Grana Padano
This cheese is similar to Parmigiano-Reggiano, but is inferior in flavour and texture. Although it is made in the same way, the milk used comes from other regions and the cheese is matured for no more than 18 months, so it does not have the crumbly texture of Reggiano and its flavour is sharper and saltier. Its grainy texture (hence the name "grana") makes it ideal for grating and it can be used for cooking in the same way as Reggiano.

SEMI-HARD CHEESE
Fontina
The only genuine Fontina comes from the Val d'Aosta in the Italian Alps, although there are plenty of poor imitations. True Fontina is made from the rich unpasteurized milk of Valdostana cows and has a fat content of 45 per cent. Although Fontina is nowadays produced on a large scale, the methods are strictly controlled and the cows are grazed only on alpine grass and herbs. Because it is matured for only about four months, the cheese has a mild, almost sweet, nutty flavour and a creamy texture, with tiny holes. Longer-matured Fontina develops a much fuller flavour and is best used for cooking. A whole Fontina weighs about 15–20kg/33– 44lb; the cheese is pale golden and the soft rind is orangey-brown. The rind of authentic Fontina has the words "Fontina dal Val d'Aosta" inscribed in white writing. Fontina is delicious eaten on its own, and because it melts beautifully and does not become stringy, it can be used instead of mozzarella in a wide variety of dishes. It is also perfect for making a fonduta, the Italian equivalent of a Swiss cheese fondue.

ABOVE: *Parmigiano Reggiano*

ABOVE: *Grana Padano*

ABOVE: *The sweet nutty flavour and creamy texture of Fontina makes it delicious to eat on its own.*

ABOVE: *Perfect to eat on its own, Taleggio has a mild, sweet flavour.*

Taleggio

A square creamy cheese from Lombardy with a fat content of almost 50 per cent, Taleggio has a mild, salty-sweet flavour, which can become pungent if it is left to age for too long (it reaches maturity after only six weeks). The cheeses are dipped in brine for about 14 hours before maturing, which gives them a slightly salty tang. Each cheese with its soft edible rind weighs about 2kg/4$\frac{1}{4}$lb. If you intend to eat the rind, remove the paper from the top! Taleggio is perfect eaten on its own as a cheese course.

SOFT CHEESES
Gorgonzola

The proper name for this famous blue-veined cheese is Stracchino Gorgonzola, because it is made from the curds of stracchino (a mild creamy cheese). Originally made only in the town of Gorgonzola, the cheese is now produced all over Lombardy. Gorgonzola is prepared by making

ABOVE: *The best mozzarella is made from buffalo milk.*

alternate layers of hot and cold curds. The best Gorgonzola cheeses are left until the mould forms naturally, but more commonly, copper wires are inserted into the cheese to encourage the growth. The cheeses are matured from three to five months; the longer the aging, the stronger the flavour.

FRESH CHEESES
Mascarpone

This delicately flavoured triple cream cheese from Lombardy is too rich to be eaten on its own (it contains 90 per cent fat), but can be used in much the same way as whipped or clotted cream and has a similar texture. It takes only 24 hours to produce, so it tastes very fresh, with a unique sweetness that makes it ideal for making desserts.

Mozzarella

Italian cooking could hardly exist without mozzarella, the pure white, egg-shaped fresh cheese, its melting quality making it perfect for so many dishes. The best mozzarella is made in the area around Naples, using water buffalo milk. Fresh mozzarella is

ABOVE: *Widely used in Italian cooking, ricotta can be combined with spinach for a ravioli filling, or used in desserts, such as cheesecake.*

delicious served in an insalata tricolore, a salad in the colours of Italy, with white mozzarella, red tomatoes and fresh green basil. Smoked mozzarella is good in sandwiches or as part of an antipasto. When cooked, mozzarella becomes uniquely stringy, so it is perfect for topping pizzas.

Ricotta

This derives its name (literally, "recooked") from the process of reheating the leftover whey from hard cheeses and adding a little fresh milk, to make a soft white curd cheese with a rather solid yet granular consistency and a fat content of only about 20 per cent. The freshly made cheeses are traditionally put into baskets to drain and take their hemispherical shape and markings from these cestelli (little baskets).

Ricotta is widely used in Italian cooking for both savoury and sweet dishes. It has an excellent texture but very little intrinsic flavour, so it makes a perfect vehicle for seasonings.

Fish and shellfish

Italy's extensive coastal waters once teemed with a huge variety of fish and shellfish, many unique to that part of the Adriatic and Mediterranean. A visit to an Italian fish market will reveal fish and shellfish of every description. Large fish are usually simply grilled (broiled) or baked and dressed with olive oil, or baked in cartoccio (enclosed in a paper bag).

Choosing fresh fish

You can almost guarantee that any fish you buy in an Italian early morning market will be ultra-fresh, but in fishmongers and restaurants you should look for pointers. Fish should have bright, slightly bulging eyes and shiny, faintly slimy skin. Open up the gills to check that they are clear red or dark pink, and prod the fish lightly to check that the flesh is springy. All fish should have only a faint, pleasant smell; you can tell a stale fish a mile off by its strong and disagreeable odour.

Red mullet (triglia)

These small Mediterranean fish rarely weigh more than 1kg/2¼lb. Red mullet (or snapper) have bright rose-coloured skin and a faint golden streak along their sides. Their flesh is succulent with a distinctive, almost prawn-like flavour, quite unlike any

ABOVE: *Red mullet has a distinctive almost prawn or shrimp-like flavour.*

other fish. The liver of red mullet is regarded as a great delicacy and is not removed during cooking, which gives the mullet its nickname of "sea woodcock". Red mullet are extremely perishable and should be eaten the day they are bought. The skin should always look very bright; dullness is a sure indication that the fish is not fresh.

Sardines (sarde)

Fresh sardines probably take their name from Sardinia, where they were once abundant. These small, silvery fish are still found in Mediterranean waters, where they grow to about 13cm/5in. They are at their best in spring. Allow about four larger

ABOVE: *Sardines combine well with tart ingredients like capers and olives.*

sardines or six smaller fish per serving. Sardines have very oily flesh and should only be eaten when extremely fresh. They can also be bought preserved in oil or salt.

Sea bass (spigola or branzino)

The silvery sea bass, which come from Mediterranean waters, are as beautiful to look at as to eat. These slim, elegant fish are almost always sold whole. Sea bass is prized for its delicate white flesh and lack of irritating small bones. As a result, it is never cheap.

Swordfish (pesce spada)

In Italy, you will occasionally find a whole swordfish on the fishmonger's slab. These huge Mediterranean fish, up to 5 metres/15 feet long and weighing 100–500kg/220–1200lb, are immediately recognizable by their long sword-like upper jaw. Because of their size, they are usually sold cut into steaks. Their firm, close-grained, almost meaty flesh has given them the nickname "steak of the sea".

ABOVE: *Swordfish needs to be marinated to keep it moist during cooking.*

ABOVE: *These smooth-shelled vongole are often steamed and served as part of a seafood salad.*

Clams (vongole)

There are almost as many different types of clam as there are regions in Italy, ranging from tiny smooth-shelled arselle or vongole, to long thin razor shells and the large Venus clams with beautiful ridged shells. All have a sweet flavour and a slightly chewy texture. They do vary in size, so it is best to ask the fishmonger how many you will need for a particular dish.

Mussels (cozze)

With their smooth texture and sweet flavour, mussels make an attractive addition to many pasta and fish dishes. Once mussels have been steamed open, they can be served with a garlicky tomato sauce, or baked on the half-shell with garlic butter or a breadcrumb topping.

Preparing mussels

Scrub the shells under cold running water. Pull away the "beard" protruding from the shell. Give any open mussels a sharp tap; they should close immediately. Discard any which do not, as they are probably dead.

ABOVE: *When small, octopus can be cooked like squid.*

Octopus (polipi))

These are much larger than squid and have only eight tentacles. Their ink sac is not located in the head but in their liver, and the ink has a strong, pungent taste. Octopuses look and taste similar to squid, but need a good deal of preparation. They must be pounded (99 times, some say) to tenderize them before they are subjected to very long, slow cooking.

Shrimps (gamberetti), prawns (gamberelli) and scampi (gamberoni)

There are so many different varieties of shrimps and prawns in Italian coastal waters that it is almost impossible to recognize them all. The smallest are the gamberetti, small pink or brown shrimps which are usually boiled and served simply dressed with olive oil and lemon juice as part of an antipasto. Next in size come the gamberelli, pink prawns with a delicate flavour. These are the prawns that are most commonly used in a fritto misto di mare (mixed fried seafood). Gamberi rossi are the larger variety of prawn, which turn bright

red when they are cooked. They are highly prized for their fine, strong flavour, and are eaten plainly cooked and dipped into a bowl of mayonnaise. Best and most expensive of all are gamberoni, large succulent prawns from the Adriatic, which have a superb flavour and texture. Similar to these is the cicala, which resembles a small flattish lobster.

Squid (calamari or totani) and cuttlefish (seppie)

Despite their appearance, squid and cuttlefish are actually molluscs, with a shell located inside the body. They are indistinguishable in taste, but cuttlefish have a larger head and a wider body with stubbier tentacles. The cuttlebone much beloved of budgerigars and parrots is the bone of the cuttlefish inside the body. Once this has been removed, cuttlefish are very tender. The "shell" of a squid is nothing more than a long, thin, transparent quill. Both seppie and calamari have ten tentacles.

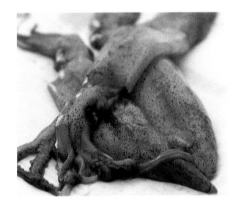

ABOVE: *Large squids like these need long, slow cooking to make them tender – conversely, small baby squid should be cooked very quickly or will become tough.*

Meat and poultry

Until recently, meat did not figure largely in Italian cooking, which relied heavily on the peasant staples of pasta, bread, vegetables. As the country became more prosperous, people added meat to their daily diet, and now animals are farmed all over Italy to provide veal, pork, beef and lamb.

Cured meats

Italy is famous for its prosciutto crudo – salted and dried ham that requires no cooking. The most famous of these hams is prosciutto di Parma, or Parma ham, which is served in wafer-thin slices. Pancetta, bresaola, mortadella and salami are also popular.

Pancetta resembles unsmoked bacon, except that it is not sold sliced, but rolled up into a sausage shape. It is made from pork belly which is cured in salt and spices.

Bresaola is often served as an antipasto, sliced very thinly and dressed with a drizzle of extra virgin oil and a sprinkling of lemon juice.

Mortadella is considered to be the finest Italian cooked sausage. It has a wonderfully smooth texture, but a rather bland flavour. It is studded with cubes of creamy fat, and often has pale green pistachios peppered throughout the meat.

There are dozens of types of salami, and their textures and flavours reflect the character and traditions of the different regions of Italy. Essentially, all salami are made from pure pork, but the finished product varies according to the kind of meat used.

Beef (manzo)

The quality of Italian beef has an unjustifiably poor reputation. It is true that in agricultural areas, particularly the south, beef can be stringy and tough. This is because the cattle are working animals, not bred for the table, and are only eaten towards the end of their hard-working life. This type of beef is only suitable for long, slow-cooked country stews. In Tuscany, however, superb beef cattle from Val di Chiana produce meat that can rival any other world-renowned beef and which provide magnificent T-bone steaks. Rump or fillet steaks are also cooked very rare and sliced on the bias as a tagliata. A modern creation is carpaccio, wafer-thin slices of raw beef marinated in olive oil and aromatics and served as an antipasto.

Lamb (abbacchio and agnello)

Lambs are bred mainly in southern Italy, particularly in the area around Rome. The youngest lamb is abbacchio, month-old milk-fed lamb from Lazio, with meltingly tender pale pinkish flesh. Abbachio is usually spit-roasted whole. Spring lamb, aged about four months, is often sold as abbacchio. It has darker flesh, which is also very tender and can be used for roasting or grilling (broiling). Older lamb (agnello) has a slightly stronger flavour and is suitable for roasting or stewing.

ABOVE: *Parma ham takes its name from the province of Parma.*

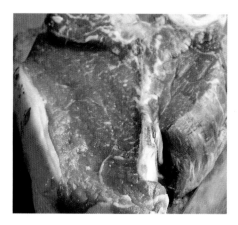

ABOVE: *Italian cooks like to grill T-bone steaks over wood fires.*

ABOVE: *A leg of darker-coloured spring lamb is perfect for roasting whole.*

ABOVE: *Tender pork chops or cutlets can be grilled (broiled) or braised with herbs.*

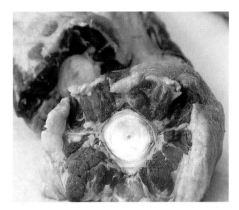

ABOVE: *Nothing is wasted in Italian butchery – oxtail is used for wonderful slow-cooked stews and soups.*

ABOVE: *Rabbit can be bought either farmed or wild – wild rabbit has a stronger flavour.*

Pork (maiale)

Most Italian pork is transformed into sausages, salami and hams, but fresh meat is enjoyed all over Italy and is often combined with local herbs like rosemary, fennel or sage. Different regions eat different parts of the pig; Tuscany is famous for its arista di maiale alla fiorentina, (loin of pork roasted with rosemary), while in Naples, il musso (the snout) is considered a great delicacy.

Offal (frattaglie)

Nothing is wasted in Italian butchery, so a huge variety of offal (innards) is available. Liver is a great favourite; the finest is fegato di vitello, tender calf's liver, which is regarded as a luxury. Chicken livers are popular for topping crostini or for pasta sauces, and pork liver is a speciality of Tuscany. Butchers often sell pig's liver ready-wrapped in natural caul (rete), which keeps the liver tender as it cooks. Lamb's and calf's kidneys (rognoni or rognoncini), brains (cervello) and sweetbreads (animelle) are specialities of northern Italy. They are

similar in texture and flavour, but sweetbreads are creamier and more delicate. Every region in Italy has its own recipes for tripe (trippa); this almost always comes from veal calves rather than other cattle, as their tripe has a coarser texture and flavour. All parts of a veal calf are considered great delicacies. The head is used in bollito misto (mixed boiled meats), and the trotters give substance to soups and stews. Oxtail (coda di bue) comes from older beef cattle.

Rabbit (coniglio) and hare (lepre)

Farmed and wild rabbits often replace chicken or veal in Italian cooking. The meat is very pale and lean, and the taste is somewhere between that of chicken and veal. Wild rabbit has a stronger flavour, which combines well with robust flavours; farmed rabbit is very tender and much more delicate. Hare cannot be farmed, so the only animals available come from the wild. The flesh is a rich, dark brown and has a strong gamey flavour.

Veal (vitello)

This is the most popular meat in Italy and appears in hundreds of different recipes. The best and most expensive veal is vitello di latte from Piedmont and Lombardy. The calves are fed only on milk and are slaughtered at just a few weeks old, producing extremely tender, very pale meat with no fat. Older calves, up to nine months old, are known as vitello. Their flesh is still tender, but darker in colour than milk-fed veal. Vitellone is somewhere between veal and beef. It comes from bullocks aged between one and three years, which have never worked in the fields; the flesh is therefore still quite tender and lighter in colour than beef.

Young, milk-fed veal is ideal for scaloppine (escalopes) and piccate (thin escalopes), which need very little cooking. Vitello can be served as chops, cutlets or a rolled roast. The shin is cut into osso buco (literally "bone with a hole"), complete with bone marrow, and braised until meltingly tender.

Cinghiale (wild boar)

Wild boar are the ancestors of the domestic pig, which used to roam in large numbers through the forests of Tuscany and Sardinia, but which are becoming increasingly rare owing to the predisposition of some Italians to shoot anything that moves. Baby wild boar are an enchanting sight, with light brown fur striped with horizontal black bands. The adults have coarse, brown coats and fierce-looking tusks. The flesh of a young boar (cinghiale) is as pale and tender as pork; older animals have very dark flesh, which is tougher but full of flavour.

Haunches of wild boar are made into hams, which are displayed in butchers' shops. Young animals can be cooked in the same way as pork. Older boar must be marinated for at least 24 hours to tenderize the meat

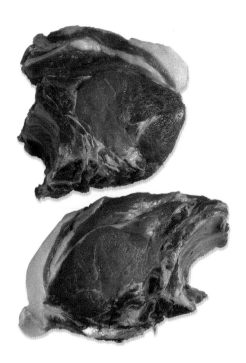

ABOVE: Wild boar chops like these can be cooked in the same way as pork.

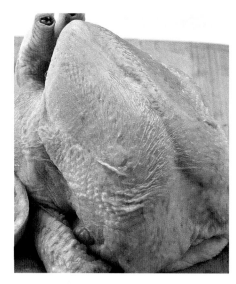

ABOVE: Chicken can be bought fresh, chilled or frozen.

before roasting or casseroling. The classic sweet and sour sauce, (agrodolce), sharpened with red wine vinegar, complements the gamey flavour of the meat.

Chicken (pollo)

Poultry is a popular food in Italy and is used to create a huge variety of simple and delicious dishes. Factory farming does exist in Italy but many flavoursome free-range birds are also available. Chicken is usually filleted for quick cooking, and removing and discarding the skin before cooking ensures the meat is lean.

Chicken is rich in high quality protein. The white meat is low in fat and contains less saturated fat than other meat.

Guinea fowl (faraona)

These are extremely decorative birds with luxuriant grey-and-white spotted plumage. They originated in West Africa, but are now farmed all over

Europe, so that, although they are technically game, they are classified as poultry. They taste similar to chicken, but have a firmer texture and a more robust flavour.

Guinea fowl are hugely popular in Italy, where they are served in much the same ways as chicken. The flesh of an adult guinea fowl is firmer than that of a chicken, so it is best to bard it with fat or cover the breasts with bacon rashers (strips) before roasting. The breasts are sometimes sautéed and served with the pan juices mixed with balsamic vinegar, or with a sauce of cream and Marsala. The birds can be roasted or pot-roasted whole, or cut into serving pieces and casseroled with mushrooms (wild mushrooms are especially delicious) or herbs. A favourite autumn dish in Tuscany is guinea fowl braised with chestnuts.

ABOVE: Guinea fowl can be pot-roasted, roasted or casseroled with wild mushrooms.

ABOVE: *Italian pheasants are less gamey than in some other countries.*

Fagiano (pheasant)

Occasionally, in the Italian countryside, you may still catch a glimpse of a pheasant with its beautiful plumage and long tail feathers. Cock pheasants have bright, iridescent blue and green feathers, while hens are browner and less dramatic-looking. Pheasant farming is still unknown in Italy, and wild pheasants are something of a rarity, so they are regarded as a luxury. They are not hung, but are eaten almost as soon as they are shot, so their flavour is less gamey than in some other countries. Although pheasants are expensive, they are meaty birds for their size, so a cock pheasant will feed three to four people and a hen pheasant, two to three.

Hen pheasants are smaller than cock birds, but their meat is juicier and the flavour is finer. Young hen pheasants can be roasted with or without a stuffing, but cock birds are more suitable for casseroling.

Pheasant breast can tend to be dry, so they should be well barded with bacon or thickly smeared with butter before roasting. A good-sized knob (pat) of butter placed inside the cavity will help to keep the flesh moist.

Pigeon (piccione)

Wood pigeons have dark, gamey flesh and a robust flavour, which the Italians love. They are generally too tough to roast, but they make the most delicious casseroles. Domestic pigeons are also reared for food, and you will often see large dovecotes in farmyards. Domestic birds are less likely to be tough than wild ones, but their flavour is less robust.

Quail (quaglie)

These small migratory birds are found in Italy throughout the summer months. Wild quails have the reputation of being so stupid that they never run away from hunters, but stay rooted to the spot as sitting targets. As a result, they have become very rare, and most of the birds now available are farmed. They are very small (you need two to serve one person) and have a delicate, subtly gamey flavour. Farmed quails have less flavour than the wild birds and benefit from added flavourings, such as grapes.

Quail should be browned in butter until golden all over, then roasted in a hot oven for about 15 minutes. Their flavour is well complemented by the fruit of the vine, so they are often served with a light sauce containing grapes or raisins soaked in grappa.

Jointing a bird

The following instructions give eight portions in total – two wings, two breasts, two thighs and two drumsticks. Use a sharp knife and poultry shears for cutting.

1 Put the bird breast-side up on a chopping board. Use a sharp knife to remove the leg by cutting through the thigh joint. Repeat on the other side.

2 Following the line of the breastbone and using poultry shears, cut the breast in half as cleanly as possible. Turn the bird over and cut out the backbone. Leave the wings attached.

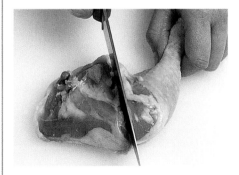

3 Cut each breast, leaving a portion of the breast attached to the wing. Then cut each leg through the knee joint to separate the thigh from the drumstick.

4 Using poultry shears, cut off the wing tip at the first joint.

Vegetables

In Italian cooking, vegetables have always played a very important role, particularly in the south of the country, where meat was a luxury that few could afford. They are most often served as dishes in their own right, rather than accompaniments, and the range of imaginative vegetable recipes from all over Italy seems infinite.

Aubergines (melanzane)

The versatile aubergine (eggplant) has a dense and satisfying texture that makes an excellent substitute for meat. You will find many different aubergines in Italian markets, the two main types being the familiar deep purple elongated variety and the rotund paler mauve type, which has a thinner skin. Some are small, some huge, but they all taste similar and can be cooked in the same way.

BELOW: *Deep purple aubergines play an important role in the cooking of southern Italy.*

Shape and size are not important when choosing aubergines; the essentials are tight, glossy skins and a fairly firm texture. Do not buy aubergines with wrinkled or damaged skins. They should feel heavy for their size; a light aubergine will probably be spongy inside and contain a lot of seeds. They will keep in the refrigerator for up to a week.

Asparagus (asparagi)

Commercially grown in north-eastern Italy for over 300 years, asparagus is still highly prized as a luxury vegetable. It has a short growing season from April to early June and is really only worth eating during this period. Both green and white asparagus are cultivated in Italy; the green variety is grown above ground so that the entire spear is bright green. They are harvested when they are about 15cm/6in high. The fat white spears with their pale yellow tips are grown under mounds of soil

BELOW: *Green asparagus is enjoyed by Italians, and can be simply boiled or roasted in olive oil.*

to protect them from the light, and harvested almost as soon as the tips appear above the soil to retain their pale colour. Both varieties have a delicious fresh grassy flavour.

Asparagus starts to lose its flavour as soon as it has been cut, so be sure to buy only the freshest spears. The best guide is the tips, which should be firm and tight. If they are drooping and open, the asparagus is past its best. The stalks should be straight and fresh-looking, not yellowed and wizened or very woody at the base. Allow about eight medium spears per serving as a first course, and always buy spears of uniform thickness so that they cook evenly.

Preparing and Cooking Asparagus

Freshly cut garden asparagus needs no trimming, but cut off at least 2cm/¾in from the bottom of the stalks of bought spears until the exposed end looks fresh and moist. Peel the lower half with a potato peeler. (You need not do this for very thin stalks.)

• Boiling asparagus can be problematical, since the stalks take longer to cook than the tips. The ideal solution is to use a special asparagus kettle, so as to immerse the stalks in boiling water whilst steaming the tips.

• Asparagus can equally well be stood upright in a deep pan of boiling water, tented with foil and cooked for 5–8 minutes, until tender but still *al dente*. Alternatively, steam the spears in a vegetable steamer. Serve with a drizzle of olive oil or butter.

ABOVE: *The name of this tall cabbage, Cavolo nero, means "black cabbage".*

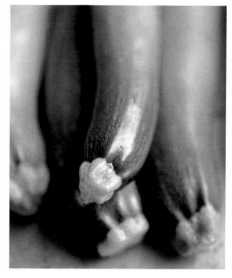

ABOVE: *Courgettes are delicious cooked simply or combined with other ingredients.*

ABOVE: *Its distinctive aniseed flavour makes fennel a perfect partner for fish.*

Cabbage (cavolo)

An essential ingredient of many hearty Italian winter soups. Three main types of cabbage are used; cavolo verza (curly-leaved savoy cabbage), which is used in Milanese dishes, cavolo cappuccio (round white or red cabbage) and the speciality of Tuscany, cavolo nero, a tall leafy cabbage which is a dark purplish green colour.

Italians rarely eat cabbage as a vegetable accompaniment, but prefer to include it in hearty soups, such as ribollita or minestrone, or to stuff and braise the outer leaves and serve them as a main course.

Cabbage heads should be solid and firm, with fresh, unyellowed leaves. It is best to buy them complete with their outer leaves; not only are these tasty for cooking, but they protect the hearts and give a good indication of the freshness of the cabbage. They will keep in the vegetable drawer of the fridge for up to a week.

Courgettes (zucchini)

These are widely used in Italy, both as a vegetable and for their deep yellow flowers. They are available all year round but are at their best in spring and summer. The smaller and skinnier the courgettes are, the better they taste. Choose courgettes that are firm with glossy green skins and avoid those which are soft or have blemished skins. Courgettes are used in many Italian dishes, and are, for example, served raw in salads, cooked with other Mediterranean vegetables such as peppers and tomatoes, or simply stuffed.

Courgettes should be firm with a glossy skin. Avoid any that feel squashy or look limp and dull.

Fennel (finocchio)

Bulb or Florence fennel (so-called to distinguish it from the feathery green herb) resembles a fat white celery root and has a delicate but distinctive flavour of aniseed and a very crisp, refreshing texture. It is delicious eaten raw, dressed with a vinaigrette or as part of a mixed salad. In southern Italy, raw fennel is served with cheese at the end of a meal.

When cooked, the aniseed flavour becomes more subtle and the texture resembles cooked celery. Fennel can be cooked in all the same ways as celery or cardoons.

Fennel is available all year round. If possible, buy it with its topknot of feathery green fronds, which you can chop and use as a herb or garnish in any dish where you would use dill. The bulbs should feel firm and the outer layers should be crisp and white, not wizened and yellowish. It should have a delicate, very fresh scent of aniseed and the crisp texture of green celery. Whole fennel bulbs will keep in the fridge for up to a week. Once cut, however, use them immediately, or the cut surfaces will discolour and the texture will soften. Allow a whole bulb per serving.

Globe artichokes (carciofi)

As their appearance suggests, artichokes are a type of thistle. Originating from Sicily, where they grow almost wild, they are cultivated throughout Italy and are a particular speciality of Roman cooking. The artichoke itself is actually the flower bud of the large, silvery-leaved plant. There are many different varieties, from tiny purple plants with tapered leaves, which are so tender that they can be eaten raw, to large bright or pale green globes.

BELOW:
Globe artichokes

Tiny tender artichokes can be quartered and eaten raw or braised alla romana with olive oil, parsley and garlic. Large specimens can be served boiled with a dressing to dip the leaves into, or stuffed with savoury fillings. They can be cut into wedges, dipped in batter and deep-fried. A favourite Italian dish is the ancient Jewish recipe carciofi alla giudea, where the artichokes are flattened out and deep-fried twice, so that the outside is very crisp while the inside remains meltingly moist.

Artichokes are available almost all year round, but they are at their best in summer. Whichever variety you are buying, look for tightly packed leaves (open leaves indicate that they are too mature) and a very fresh colour. When an artichoke is old, the tips of the leaves will turn brown. If possible, buy artichokes still attached to their stems; they will remain fresher and the peeled, cooked stems are often as delicious as the artichoke itself.

Artichokes will keep fresh for several days if you place the stalks in water like a bunch of flowers. If they have no stalks, wrap them in clear film (plastic wrap) and keep in the refrigerator for a day or two.

ABOVE: *A few dried porcini make a delicious addition to ordinary fresh mushrooms, giving them a flavour of wild mushrooms.*

Mushrooms (funghi)

The most highly-prized mushroom for use in Italian cooking is the porcino (cep). As these are hugely expensive, they are most often dried and used in small quantities to add flavour to field or other wild mushrooms. Drying intensifies the flavour of porcini, so they are not regarded as inferior to the fresh mushrooms. Other popular wild fungi include gallinacci (chanterelles), prataioli (field (portabello) mushroooms) and ovoli (Caesar's mushrooms).

Preparing globe artichokes

For large artichokes, snap off the stalk and pull off the tough leaves. Rub lemon juice into the cut surfaces to prevent discoloration. Keep in a bowl of acidulated water until ready to cook.
• Very small artichokes only need to be quartered and cooked until tender.

• Boil large whole artichokes for about 30 minutes, until the outer leaves can be pulled off easily. Drain and pull out the centre leaves and scoop out the inedible hairy choke with a spoon.
• For stuffed artichokes, remove the choke before cooking and fill the cavity with your chosen stuffing, cover with foil and bake in the oven.

ABOVE: *Chanterelles look pretty and have a wonderful flavour.*

ABOVE: *Yellow onions are mild, and are best cooked gently in olive oil.*

ABOVE: *Baby white onions are traditionally cooked in agrodolce, a classic Italian sauce, and served as an antipasto.*

Never store mushrooms in a plastic bag, as they will sweat and turn mushy. Put them into a paper bag and keep in the refrigerator for no more than two days.

Cultivated mushrooms and ceps can be eaten raw, but other edible wild mushrooms should be cooked before eating. In Italy, mushrooms may simply be lightly grilled (broiled) or baked or added to many dishes, such as sauces, stocks, soups and risottos.

Mushrooms should not be washed or they will become waterlogged and mushy. To clean them, cut off the earthy base of the stalk and wipe them clean with a damp cloth.

Onions (cipolle)

These are an essential part of Italian cooking. Many varieties are grown, including mild yellow onions. The stronger-flavoured white onions and their baby version are used for pickling and sweet-and-sour onions. The best-known Italian onions are the vibrant deep red variety, which are delicious raw, in a tuna and bean salad, for example, or cooked.

The best Italian onions are grown in Piedmont, so many classic Piedmontese recipes include these versatile bulbs. Large onions can be stuffed with Fontina or minced (ground) meat and herbs, and baked.

Baby white onions are traditionally cooked in agrodolce, a sweet-and-sour sauce of sugar and wine vinegar, and served cold as an antipasto or hot as a vegetable accompaniment.

You will often find young fresh onions in Italian markets. These are sold in bunches like large, bulbous spring onions, complete with their leaves. They have a mild flavour and can be used for pickling or in salads. They will keep in the vegetable drawer in the refrigerator for three or four days; wrap them tightly to stop their smell pervading everything else in the refrigerator.

Older onions have thin, almost papery skins that should be unblemished. The onions should feel firm and not be sprouting green leaves. They quickly deteriorate once cut, so it is best to buy assorted sizes, then you can use a small onion when the recipe calls for only a small amount. Stored in a dry, airy place, onions will keep for many weeks.

Reconstituting dried mushrooms

Soak 25 g/1 oz dried mushrooms in 250 ml/8 fl oz/1 cup hot water for about 20 minutes until soft, then drain and use like fresh mushrooms. Keep the soaking water to use in sauces, stocks or soups; it will have an intense mushroom flavour.

Peppers (peperoni)

Generically known as capsicums, the shape of these sweet peppers gives them the alternative name of "bell peppers". Although they come in a range of colours – green (these are unripe red peppers), red, yellow, orange and even purplish-black – all peppers have much the same sweetish flavour and crunchy texture, and are interchangeable in recipes. They are a very healthy food, being rich in vitamin C.

Each region of Italy has its own specialities using peppers. They can be used raw or lightly roasted in salads or as an antipasto, and can be cooked in a variety of ways. Peppers go well with other Mediterranean ingredients, such as olives, capers, aubergines (eggplants), tomatoes and anchovies.

Choose firm peppers with shiny, unwrinkled skins. Size does not matter unless you plan to stuff the peppers, in which case choose roundish shapes of uniform size. The skin of green peppers may be mottled with patches of orange or red; this indicates that the pepper is ripening.

BELOW: *Locally grown Italian peppers are often larger and more misshapen than the uniformly perfect ones grown in hot-houses.*

ABOVE: Radicchio di Treviso *is delicious grilled with olive oil.*

Radicchio

This variety of red-leafed chicory comes originally from Treviso. Radicchio di Treviso has elongated purplish-red leaves with pronounced cream-coloured veins. The more familiar round variety is known as radicchio di Verona. Both types of red-leafed chicory have a bitter taste, and for salads are best used in small quantities together with other leaves. They look particularly attractive when combined with frilly-leafed curly endive, pale whitish-green chicory leaves, or the darker corn-salad and rocket (arugula). Radicchio can also be eaten as a hot vegetable.

Rocket (rucola)

Also known as arugula, this vegetable has dark green elongated, indented leaves and a hot, pungent flavour and aroma. It grows wild in the Italian countryside, but it is also cultivated commercially. Home-grown rocket has a much better flavour than the leaves usually found in supermarkets.

ABOVE: *A hot, pungent salad leaf, rocket grows wild in the Italian countryside.*

Rocket adds zest to any green salad and can be eaten on its own with a dressing of olive oil and lemon juice or balsamic vinegar. Combined with radicchio, cornsalad and fresh herbs, rocket makes a good substitute for misticanza. It can be added to pasta sauces and risotti, or cooked like spinach, but cooking does diminish the pungent flavour.

Rocket does not keep well unless it has been pre-packaged. To keep it for a day or two, wrap it in damp newspaper or damp kitchen paper and store in the refrigerator.

Cooking peppers

To make a classic Italian peperonata, sweat sliced onions and garlic in olive oil, add sliced (bell) peppers, cover the pan and cook gently until just tender. Add an equal quantity of peeled, deseeded and chopped tomatoes, a splash of wine vinegar and seasoning and cook, uncovered, until meltingly tender. For peperonata alla romana, stir in some capers at the end.

Tomatoes (pomodori)

It is impossible to imagine Italian cooking without tomatoes, which seem to be a vital ingredient in almost every recipe.

Tomatoes are used in so many different ways that it is hard to know where to begin. They can be eaten raw, sliced and served with a trickle of extra virgin olive oil and some torn basil leaves (basil and tomatoes have an extraordinary affinity). They are the red component of an insalata tricolore, partnering white mozzarella and green basil to make up the colours of the Italian flag. Raw ripe tomatoes can be chopped with herbs and garlic to make a fresh-tasting pasta sauce, or made into a topping for bruschetta.

Tomatoes can be grilled, fried, baked, stuffed, stewed and made into sauces and soups. They add colour and flavour to any savoury dish. Tomatoes are at their best in summer, when they have ripened naturally in the sun. Choose your tomatoes according to how you wish to prepare them. Salad tomatoes should be very firm and easy to slice. The best tomatoes for cooking are the plum

BELOW: *San Marzano are the best variety of plum tomatoes.*

ABOVE: *Tomatoes sold on the vine are likely to have a far better flavour than those sold loose.*

tomatoes, which hold their shape well and should have a fine flavour.

Tomatoes will only ripen properly if left for long enough on the vine, so try to buy "vine-ripened" varieties. If you can find only unripe tomatoes, you can ripen them by putting them in a brown paper bag with a ripe tomato or leaving them in a fruit bowl with a banana; the gases the ripe fruits give off will ripen the tomatoes, but, alas, they cannot improve the flavour.

Try to buy tomatoes loose so that you can smell them. They should have a wonderful aroma. If the flavour is not all it should be, add a good pinch of sugar to enhance it. For cooked recipes, if you cannot find really flavourful tomatoes, use canned instead. The best are San Marzano plum tomatoes, which are grown near Salerno. In Italy, you will often find large knobbly green tomatoes, which are sold as pomodori insalata. Although you can allow them to ripen in the usual way, Italians prefer to slice these tomatoes thinly and eat them in their unripe state as a crunchy and refreshing salad.

Basic tomato sauce

Makes about 600ml/1 pint/2½ cups

900g/2lb fresh tomatoes, skinned and
    quartered, or 2 x 400g/14oz cans
    tomatoes, drained and quartered
1 small onion, quartered
1 carrot, quartered
1 celery stick, quartered
1 large parsley sprig
10 fresh basil leaves
sea salt
45ml/3 tbsp extra virgin olive oil (optional)

1 Put the tomatoes, onion, carrot, celery, parsley and basil into a pan. Cover and bring to the boil, then simmer for 30 minutes.

2 Remove the lid and continue to simmer for a further 20 minutes, or until most of the liquid has evaporated.

3 Remove from the heat and push the mixture through a food mill or sieve (strainer). Season to taste with salt, and reheat, adding the oil, if using, just before serving, or using in a recipe.

• To skin tomatoes: plunge the tomatoes into boiling water for 30 seconds, then refresh in cold water. Peel away the skins.

Fruit

Italy produces an abundance of soft, stone and citrus fruits, all bursting with flavour and often available fresh from the tree. There are apples and pears from the orchards of the northern regions; peaches, plums and figs from the central plains; while the south and Sicily produce almost every kind of fruit – grapes, cherries, oranges and lemons.

After a full meal of antipasto, pasta and a secondo (main course), it is hardly surprising that Italian desserts very often consist of nothing but a bowl of seasonal fresh fruit served on its own or made into a refreshing macedonia (fruit salad). Soft fruits form the basis of many delicious ice creams, sorbets, granite and frullati (fresh fruit milkshakes).

Fig (fico)
These are grown all over Italy, but thanks to the hot climate, Sicilian figs are perhaps the most luscious of all. During the summer months you will often find Italian farmers at the roadside selling punnets of ripe figs from their own trees. There are two types of Italian figs, green and purple. Both have thin, tender skins and very sweet, succulent, red flesh, and are rich in vitamins A, B and C. They are in season from July to October and are best eaten straight from the tree when they are perfectly ripe.

ABOVE: *The sweet succulent flesh of purple figs makes a perfect partner to nuts of all kinds.*

Fresh figs are delicious served on their own, but they have an affinity with nuts such as walnuts, pistachios and almonds. They can be served raw with prosciutto or salami as an antipasto, or stuffed with raspberry coulis or mascarpone as a dessert. Poached in a little water or wine flavoured with cinnamon or nutmeg, they make an excellent accompaniment to duck, game or lamb.

Ripe figs are extremely delicate and do not travel well, so it is hard to find imported fruit at a perfect stage of maturity. In season in Italy, however, you can find local figs that are just ripe for eating; they should be soft and yielding, but not squashy. Sometimes the skin may have split, revealing the luscious red or pink flesh. As long as you are going to eat the fig immediately, this does not matter.

Under-ripe figs can be kept at room temperature for a day or two until the skin softens, but they will never develop the fine flavour of tree-ripened figs. Ripe figs should be eaten on the day they are bought.

Fresh figs are low in calories, and are rich in vitamins A, E and K, minerals and antioxidants, as well as being a good source of beneficial soluble fibre.

Preparing figs
Wash the figs briefly and gently pat dry. Discard the stalk and peel the figs, if you wish.
• To serve as an antipasto or dessert, cut them downwards from the stalk end into quarters, leaving them attached at the base. Open them out like flowers.
• Perfectly ripe figs are best eaten raw, but less perfect specimens can be improved by cooking. They can be gently poached in syrup or red wine flavoured with a cinnamon stick or vanilla pod, or rolled in caster sugar and baked in the oven until caramelized. Barely ripe figs also make excellent jam.

Grapes (uva)

Italy is the world's largest producer of grapes of all kinds. Almost every rural property boasts an expanse of vineyards, some producing wine-making grapes intended only for home consumption. Others (particularly in Chianti and the south) are destined for the enormous Italian wine-making industry. Apulia, Abruzzo and Sicily produce sweet dessert grapes on a vast commercial scale, from large luscious Italia, with their fine muscat flavour, to Cardinal, named for its deep red colour, purple Alphonse Lavallé, and various small seedless varieties.

Despite their high calorific value, grapes are extremely good for you, since they are rich in potassium, iron and vitamins.

Choosing white, black or red grapes is a matter of preference; beneath the skin, the flesh is always pale green and juicy. Buy bunches of grapes with fruit which is of equal size and not too densely packed on the stalk. Check that none is withered or bad. The skin should have a delicate bloom and be firm to the touch. Try to eat one grape from a bunch to see how they taste. The flesh should be firm and very juicy and refreshing. Grapes should be washed immediately after purchase, then placed in a bowl and kept in the refrigerator for up to three days.

Lemon (limone)

These are grown all over Italy, even in the northern regions. Lake Garda boasts a town called Limone, named for its abundance of lemon trees. The most famous Italian lemons come from the Amalfi coast, where they grow to an extraordinary size and have such a sweet flavour that they can almost be eaten as a dessert fruit. Their aromatic flavour enhances almost any dish, and they have the added advantage of being rich in vitamin C.

Lemons are a key ingredient in many dishes because of their versatility. The juice can be squeezed to make a refreshing spremuta di limone, or it can be added to other cold drinks or tea. It is an anti-oxidant, which prevents discoloration when applied to other cut fruits and vegetables. The juice is used for dressings and for flavouring all sorts of drinks and sauces. A squeeze of lemon juice adds a different dimension to intrinsically bland foods, such as fish, poultry, veal or certain vegetables. Its acidity also helps to bring out the flavour of other fruits.

RIGHT: *Lemons are grown all over Italy, where the aromatic flavour in both the juice and rind is used to enhance many dishes, both sweet and savoury..*

Preparing lemons

Before squeezing a lemon, warm it gently: either put it in a bowl, pour boiling water over the top and leave to stand for about 5 minutes or, if you prefer, microwave the lemon on full power for about 30 seconds; this will significantly increase the quantity of juice you will obtain.

• For sweet dishes, when you want to add the flavour of lemons, but not the grated rind, rub a sugar lump over the skin of the lemon to absorb the oil, then use the sugar as part of the recipe.

• To prepare grated lemon rind, thoroughly wash and dry unwaxed lemons. Grate the rind or peel it off with a zester, taking care not to include any white pith.

Melon (melone)

Many different varieties of sweet, aromatic melons are grown in Italy, and each has its own regional name. Napoletana melons have a smooth pale green rind and delicately scented orange flesh. Cantalupo (cantaloupe) melons have a warty skin, which is conveniently marked into segments, and highly scented deep yellow flesh. A similar Tuscan melon with grey-green rind and orange flesh is called popone. These melons are all perfect for eating with prosciutto or salami as an antipasto.

Watermelons (anguria or cocomero) are grown in Tuscany. These huge green melons with their refreshing bright pink or red flesh and edible brown seeds can be round or sausage-shaped.

Italians eat melon as a starter, usually accompanied by wafer-thin prosciutto crudo or cured meats. Melons and watermelons are occasionally served as a dessert fruit on their own, but more often appear in a macedonia (fruit salad).

The best way to tell whether a melon is ripe is to smell it; it should have a mild, sweet scent. If it smells highly perfumed and musky, it will be over-ripe. The fruit should feel heavy for its size and the skin should not be bruised or damaged. Gently press the rind with your thumbs at the stalk end; it should give a little. Melons will ripen quickly at room temperature and should be eaten within two or three days. Wrap cut melon tightly in clear film (plastic wrap) before storing in the refrigerator, or its scent may permeate other foods.

Morello cherry (amarena)

Although Italy does produce sweet dessert cherries, it is best known for the bitter Morello variety, which are preserved in syrup or brandy, or made into ice cream and Maraschino liqueur. These cherries are small, with dark red skins and firm flesh. They are in season from late June to early July, and can be eaten raw, although they have quite a sharp flavour.

ABOVE: *Morello cherries are usually preserved in syrup and used for desserts. Those bottled in vinegar can be used for savoury recipes.*

Morello cherries can be poached in sugar syrup and served whole, or puréed and made into a rich, dark, cherry syrup; they also make an excellent jam.

Choose fresh cherries with unwrinkled and unblemished skins, which look shiny and feel firm. Stored in a plastic bag, they will keep in the refrigerator for up to a week.

Orange (arancia)

Many varieties of oranges are grown in Sicily and southern Italy. The best-known Sicilian oranges are the small blood oranges with their bright ruby-red flesh. Other types of sweet oranges include seedless navels, which take their name from the umbilical-like end which contains an embryonic orange, and seeded late oranges, which have paler flesh and are available throughout the winter. Bitter oranges are also grown; these rough-skinned varieties are made into preserves, candied peel and liquore all'arancia (orange liqueur).

RIGHT: *The sweet scented flesh of Napoletana melon, and the similar cantaloupe melon, is perfect for eating with prosciutto as an antipasto.*

LEFT: *Occasionally served on its own in wedges as a dessert, watermelon is usually chopped and added to a fruit salad.*

A favourite Sicilian recipe is insalata di arance alla siciliana, a salad of thinly sliced oranges and red onion rings, dressed with black olives and their oil. Oranges also combine well with raw fennel and chicory. They can be sliced and served alla veneziana, coated with caramel, or simply macerated in a little lemon juice with a sliver of lemon peel for a refreshing dessert. They can be squeezed for juice, or made into sorbet and granita. Bitter oranges combine well with white fish, calf's liver, duck or game, and add zest to a tomato sauce.

Oranges are available all year round, but are at their best in winter. They should have unblemished shiny skins and feel heavy for their size (this indicates that they contain plenty of juice and that the flesh is not dry). If you intend to candy the peel or incorporate it into a recipe, choose unwaxed oranges. Oranges will keep at room temperature for a week and for at least two weeks in the refrigerator. Bring them back to room temperature or warm them slightly before eating them.

ABOVE: *Sweet varieties of orange are used for both sweet and savoury recipes – they are a favourite addition to salads.*

ABOVE: *Peaches are grown in central and southern Italy.*

Peaches (pesche) and nectarines (pesche noci)

Peaches, with their velvety skin and sweet, juicy flesh, are a summer fruit grown in central and southern Italy. The most common variety is the pesca gialla (yellow peach), which has succulent, yellow flesh. More highly prized are the pesche bianche (white peaches), with pink-tinted flesh that is full of juice and flavour.

Nectarines have smooth plum-like skins and taste very similar to peaches. They also come in yellow and white varieties and, like peaches, the white nectarines have a finer flavour. Some people prefer nectarines as a dessert fruit because they do not require peeling. Peaches and nectarines are interchangeable in cooked dishes.

Peaches and nectarines are delicious served as a dessert fruit, but can also be macerated in fortified wine or spirits, or poached in white wine and syrup. They have a particular affinity with almonds. They are also delicious served with raspberries, or made into fruit drinks, ice creams and sorbets.

ABOVE: *Nectarines are delicious served as a dessert fruit.*

Peaches are in season from June to September. Make sure they are ripe, but not too soft, with unwrinkled and unblemished skins. They should have a sweet, intense scent. Peaches and nectarines bruise very easily, so try to buy those that have been kept in compartmented trays rather than piled into punnets.

Do not keep peaches and nectarines for more than a day or two. If they are very juicy and ripe, store them in the refrigerator.

Preparing peaches

To peel peaches, place them in a heatproof bowl and pour boiling water over them. Leave for 15–30 seconds (depending on how ripe they are), then refresh in very cold water; the skins will slip off easily.

Nuts

Many different kinds of nuts are grown in Italy – chestnuts and hazelnuts in the north, pine nuts in the coastal regions, and almonds, pistachios and walnuts in the south. They are used in a wide variety of savoury dishes, cakes and pastries, or served as a dessert with a glass of vin santo (sweet white wine).

Almonds (mandorle)

Two varieties of almonds are grown in central and southern Italy. Mandorle dolci (sweet almonds) are eaten as a dessert or used in cooking and baking, while mandorle amare (bitter almonds) are used to flavour liqueurs like amaretto or bittersweet confections such as amaretti bicuits. These almonds are not edible in their raw state; in fact, they are poisonous if consumed in large quantities. Both types of almonds have a velvety pale green outer casing; the hard light brown shell within encloses one or two oval nuts.

ABOVE: *In Italy in early spring, fresh almonds are eaten raw as a dessert.*

ABOVE: *Chestnuts are a mainstay of Tuscan and Sardinian cooking.*

Early in the season (late May), sweet almonds can be eaten raw as a dessert. They have a delicious fresh flavour and the brown skin is still soft enough to be palatable. Later, dried sweet almonds are blanched, slivered or ground to be used for cakes, pastries and all sorts of confectionery, including marzapane (marzipan) and croccante (almond brittle). They can be devilled or salted as an appetizing snack with an aperitif. Toasted almonds are the classic garnish for trout, and go well with chicken or rabbit. Dried bitter almonds are used in small quantities to add a more intense flavour to biscuits and cakes.

Chestnuts (castagne)

These are a mainstay of Tuscan and Sardinian cooking, dating back to the days when the peasants could not afford wheat to make flour, so they ground up the chestnuts that grow in abundance throughout the region instead. Most varieties of sweet chestnut contain two or three nuts inside the spiky green husk, but commercially grown varieties contain a single, large nut, which is easier to peel and better for roasting.

Chestnuts have shiny, rich reddish-brown shells with a wrinkled, thin skin beneath, which can be very hard to remove. They cannot be eaten raw, but once cooked, the starchy nuts are highly nutritious and very sustaining. The nicest chestnuts are those you gather yourself, but if you are buying them, look for large, shiny specimens, with no tiny holes in the shells. The chestnuts should feel heavy for their size and not rattle when you shake them. They will keep in a cool place for at least two weeks. If any holes appear in the shells, discard the nut.

Hazelnuts (nocciole)

Fresh hazelnuts are harvested in August and September, and during these months are always sold in their frilled green husks. The small round nuts have a very sweet flavour and a milky texture when fresh. In Italy, they are generally dried and used in confectionery and cakes.

Hazelnuts are used in all sorts of confectionery, including torrone (a sort of nougat) and gianduiotti, a delicious fondant chocolate from Piedmont. The famous chocolate baci ("kisses") from Perugia contain a whole hazelnut in the centre.

ABOVE: *When fresh, hazelnuts have a very sweet flavour.*

Hazelnuts are finely ground to make cakes and biscuits, and are excellent in stuffings for poultry and game. If hazelnuts are sold in their fresh green husks, you can be sure they are fresh and juicy. Otherwise, look for shiny shells which are not too thick and unblemished; cracked shells will cause the nut to shrivel and dry out. Shelled hazelnuts should be kept in an airtight container for no longer than one month.

Pine nuts (pinoli)

The kernels or nuts are actually the seeds from the stone pine trees that grow in profusion along the Adriatic and Mediterranean coasts of Italy. The small, rectangular, cream-coloured seeds grow inside a hard husk and are extracted from between the scales of the pine cones. The soft-textured kernels, which have an oily, slightly resinous flavour, are always sold de-husked. They can be eaten raw, but are usually toasted before use to bring out the flavour.

ABOVE: *The oily, slightly resinous flavour of pine nuts is accentuated by toasting.*

ABOVE: *Pistachios have a mild yet distinctive flavour.*

Pine nuts are used in many Italian dishes, both sweet and savoury, but they are best known as an essential ingredient of pesto. They go well with meat and game, and make delicious biscuits (cookies) and tarts.

Pine nuts are always sold out of the husk. Because they are very oily, they go rancid quite quickly. Store them in an airtight container in the refrigerator for not more than a week.

Pistachios (pistacchi)

Native to the Near East, pistachios are grown in southern Italy, particularly in Sicily. The small, bright green nut has a yellowish-red skin and is enclosed in a smooth, pale shell. Pistachios have a sweet, delicate flavour, which makes them ideal for desserts, but they are also used to stud mortadella and other pale cooked meat products.

Pistachios can be eaten raw or roasted and salted as a snack with an aperitivo. Their colour enhances most white meats and poultry. They make deliciously rich ice cream and are used in cassata gelata, the famous Sicilian dessert.

If possible, buy pistachios still in their shells. These will be easier to open if they are already slightly ajar; once open, the nut is very easy to remove. Shelled, blanched pistachios are also available. They are useful for cooking, but lack the fine flavour of whole nuts. Store blanched pistachios in an airtight container for up to two weeks. Whole nuts will keep for well over a month.

Walnuts (noci)

These grow in abundance throughout central and southern Italy. The kernels, shaped like the two halves of a brain, grow inside a pale brown, heavily indented shell enclosed by a smooth green fleshy husk or "shuck". Fresh walnuts have a delicious milky sweetness and a soft texture, which hardens as the nuts mature.

Walnuts can be ground or chopped and used in cakes and desserts, and used to make savoury sauces for pasta. Walnut oil has a distinctive flavour and makes an excellent salad dressing. They will keep for at least two months. Never store walnuts in the refrigerator, as the oil they contain will harden and ruin the flavour.

ABOVE: *In Italy, fresh walnuts are often eaten straight from the shell as a dessert.*

Herbs and flavourings

Herbs are vital to Italian cooking. Their flavour adds depth and interest to what is essentially plain cooking, based on fresh ingredients. It is impossible to imagine roast chicken or veal without rosemary or sage, or pesto or tomatoes without basil.

Basil (basilico)

With its intense aroma and fresh, pungently sweet flavour, basil is associated with Italian cooking more than any other herb. It is an essential ingredient of pesto, but it also finds its way into soups, salads and almost all dishes based on tomatoes, with which it has an extraordinary affinity. There are over 50 varieties of this herb, but the one most commonly used in Italy is sweet basil, with its fresh green leaves and wonderfully spicy aroma.

Basil has a volatile flavour, so it is best added to dishes at the end of cooking. It can be used in any dish that contains tomatoes, and is

delicious sprinkled on to a pizza. It adds a pungent, sweet note to almost all salads and is particularly good with white fish and seafood. It makes an excellent flavouring for omelettes and is often added to minestrone. The most famous of all basil dishes is pesto, the fragrant Genoese sauce made by pounding together fresh basil, garlic, Parmesan, pine nuts and olive oil.

Marjoram (maggiorana) and oregano (origano)

These two highly aromatic herbs are closely related (oregano is the wild variety), but marjoram has a much milder flavour. Marjoram is more commonly used in northern Italy, while oregano is widely used in the south to flavour tomato dishes, vegetables and pizzas. Drying greatly intensifies the flavour of both herbs, so they should be used very sparingly. In northern Italy, sweet marjoram is used to flavour meat, poultry,

vegetables and soups; the flavour goes particularly well with carrots and cucumber. Despite its rather pungent aroma, marjoram has a delicate flavour, so it should be added to long-cooked foods towards the end of cooking.

Oregano is used exclusively in southern Italian cooking, especially in tomato-based dishes. It is a classic flavouring for pizza, but should always be used in moderation.

ABOVE: *Basil is widely associated with Italian cooking.*

BELOW: *The aromatic flavour of marjoram is very similar to that of oregano, but much milder.*

Making pesto

This will make enough pesto for about 4–6 servings of pasta.

1 put 115g/4oz basil leaves in a mortar with 25g/1oz pine nuts, 2 fat peeled garlic cloves and a large pinch of coarse salt, and crush to a paste with a pestle.

2 Work in 50g/2oz freshly grated Parmesan. Gradually add about 120ml/4fl oz extra virgin olive oil, working it in thoroughly with a wooden spoon to make a thick, creamy sauce.

3 Put the pesto in a jar; it will keep for several weeks in the refrigerator.

ABOVE: *Italian parsley is the flat leafed variety. It has a strong, robust flavour.*

ABOVE : *The flavour of rosemary is intensified when it is dried.*

ABOVE : *There are several varieties of sage grown in the Italian countryside.*

Parsley (prezzemolo)

Italian parsley is of the flat leaf variety, which has a more robust flavour than curly parsley. It has attractive dark green leaves, which resemble coriander (cilantro). It is used as a flavouring in innumerable cooked dishes, but rarely as a garnish. If flat leaf parsley is not available, curly parsley makes a perfectly adequate substitute. Parsley is an extremely nutritious herb, rich in iron and potassium and vitamin C.

Parsley can be used to flavour innumerable savoury dishes. It adds colour and flavour to sauces, soups and risotti. The stalks can be used to flavour stocks and stews. Chopped parsley can be sprinkled over cooked savoury dishes; whole leaves are rarely used as a garnish in Italy.

Rosemary (rosmarino)

Spiky evergreen rosemary bushes, with their attractive blue flowers, grow wild all over Italy. The herb has a delicious, highly aromatic flavour, which is intensifed when it is dried.

The texture of rosemary leaves is quite hard and the taste is very pungent, so it is never used raw, but is excellent for cooking. Its flavour can easily overpower a dish, so make sure you only use a few leaves in a dish.

Rosemary combines extremely well with roast or grilled lamb, veal and chicken. A few needles will enhance the flavour of baked fish or any tomato dish, and it adds a wonderful flavour to roast potatoes and onions. Some rosemary branches added to the charcoal on a barbecue impart a superb flavour to whatever is being cooked. Dried rosemary can always be substituted for fresh; it is extremely pungent, so should be used sparingly.

Sage (salvia)

Wild sage grows in profusion in the Italian countryside. There are several varieties, including the common garden sage, with furry silvery-grey leaves and spiky purple flowers, and clary sage, with hairy curly leaves, which is used to make dry vermouth. All sages have a slightly bitter aromatic flavour, which contrasts well with fatty meats such as pork. In northern Italy, particularly Tuscany, it is used to flavour veal and chicken.

Sage combines well with almost all meat and vegetable dishes and is often used in minestrone. It has a particular affinity with veal (such as osso buco, piccata and, of course, calf's liver) and is an essential ingredient of saltimbocca alla romana, veal escalopes and prosciutto crudo topped with sage leaves.

Capers (capperi)

These are the immature flower buds of a wild Mediterranean shrub. They are pickled in white wine vinegar or preserved in brine, which gives them a piquant, peppery flavour. Sicilian capers are packed in whole salt, which should be rinsed off before using the capers. Bottled nasturtium flower buds are sometimes sold as a cheaper alternative to true capers. Caper berries look like large, fat capers on a long stalk, but they are actually the fruit of the caper shrub.

Chillies (peperoncini)

Chopped fresh chillies or hot flakes of dried chillies are added to many low-fat Italian dishes. Fresh chillies vary in taste from mild to fiery hot, and they are unusual in that their "hotness" is usually in inverse proportion to their size, so larger, round fleshly varieties are generally milder than the smaller, thin-skinned pointed ones. For a milder spicy flavour, remove and discard the seeds and veins from fresh chillies before use. A small pinch of dried chilli flakes spices up low-fat stews and sauces, particularly those made with tomatoes. For a really hot low-fat pizza, crumble a few dried chilli flakes over the top. Dried chillies are extremely fiery and should be used sparingly.

Take care when preparing fresh chillies and always wear rubber or plastic gloves, or wash your hands and utensils thoroughly after use, as chillies contain volatile oils which can irritate and burn if they touch sensitive areas, especially the eyes.

ABOVE: *Dried chillies are often used in fiery southern Italian dishes, such as arrabbiata sauce.*

ABOVE: *The purple-skinned garlic has a more delicate taste than the white variety.*

Garlic (aglio)

This is not, as you might suppose, a type of onion, but is a member of the lily family. The bulb or "head" is a collection of cloves held together by a papery white or purplish skin. When crushed or chopped it releases a pungent, slightly acrid oil with a very distinctive flavour and smell. Freshly picked garlic is milder than older, dried garlic, and the large, mauve-tinged variety has a more delicate flavour than the smaller white variety.

Garlic finds its way into many Italian dishes, but it is generally used with discretion so as not to flavour the food too aggressively.

It can be roasted with lamb and potatoes, or baked in its skin for a mellower flavour. Blanched, crushed garlic will aromatize olive oil to make a good dressing for salads or to use in cooking where only a hint of garlic flavour is required. Raw skinned garlic cloves can be rubbed over toasted croûtons to make flavourful bruschetta bases.

ABOVE: *Black olives are grown all over Italy and have a strong, salty flavour.*

Olives (olive)

A wide variety of olives are cultivated all over Italy. Most are destined to be pressed into oil, but some are kept as table olives to be salted, pickled or marinated, and served as part of an antipasto or used in cooking. There are two main types, green (immature) and black (mature); both are bitter and inedible in their natural state.

Green olives are the unripe fruit, which are picked in October or November. They have a sharper flavour and crunchier texture than black olives, which continue to ripen on the tree and are not harvested until December. Among the best Italian table olives are the small, shiny black Gaeta olives from Liguria. Wrinkled black olives from Lazio have a strong, salty flavour, while Sardinian olives are semi-ripened and are brown or purplish in colour. The largest olives come from Apulia and Sicily, where giant, green specimens are grown. These may be stoned (pitted) and stuffed with pimento, anchovy or almonds. Cured olives can be flavoured with garlic, local herbs, orange or lemon zest and dried chillies.

Olives can be served on their own or as a garnish or topping for pizza. They combine well with ingredients like tomatoes, aubergines (eggplants), anchovies and capers and are used in sauces for rabbit, chicken and firm-fleshed fish. Made into a paste with red wine vinegar, garlic and olive oil, they make an excellent topping for crostini.

ABOVE: *Saffron imparts a wonderfully rich yellow colour to dishes such as risotto.*

Saffron (zafferano)
This vivid spice consists of the dried stigmas of the saffron crocus. It takes around 80,000 crocuses to produce about 500g/1¼lb of spice and these have to be hand-picked, so it is hardly surprising that saffron is the world's most expensive spice. Saffron stigmas or threads are a orangey-red colour with a pungent aroma. They are also sold ground into powder. Saffron has a highly aromatic flavour and will impart a wonderful, rich golden colour to risotti and sauces.

Olive oil (olio di oliva)
Unlike other oils, which are extracted from the seeds or dried fruits of plants, olive oil is pressed from the pulp of ripe olives, which gives it an inimitable richness and flavour. Different regions of Italy produce distinctively different olive oils; Tuscan oil (considered the best) is pungent and peppery, Ligurian oil is lighter and sweeter, while the oils from the south and Sicily are powerful and nutty.

The best olive oil is extra virgin, which is strictly controlled and regulated like wine. This is made simply by pressing the olives to extract the oil, with no further processing. Extra virgin olive oil must have an acidity level of less than 1 per cent. The distinctive fruity flavour of this oil makes it ideal for dressings and using raw. Virgin olive oil is pressed in the same way, but has a higher acidity level and a less refined flavour. It, too, can be used as a condiment, but is also suitable for cooking. Unclassified olive oil is refined, then blended with virgin oil to add flavour. It has an undistinguished taste, but is ideal for cooking; it should not be used as a condiment.

For cooking, pure olive oil is fine. Once opened, olive oil should be kept in a cool place away from the light. The best oil will soon lose its savour, so use it within six months.

RIGHT: *Extra virgin olive oil has a distinctive fruity flavour, making it ideal for dressings.*

RIGHT: *Sun-dried tomatoes are available dry in packets or preserved in oil.*

Sun-dried Tomatoes (pomodori secchi)
Wrinkled red sun-dried tomatoes are available dry in packets or preserved in oil in jars. Dry-packed tomatoes are lower in fat than the oil-packed ones and are used in many low-fat Italian dishes to add flavour and colour. They can be eaten on their own as a snack, or soaked in hot water until soft, then added to numerous dishes including sauces, soups, egg and vegetable dishes.

They make an excellent antipasto combined with sliced fresh tomatoes, mozzarella and basil. Use the oil in which the tomatoes are preserved for salad dressings. The paste can be used in small quantities for sauces and soups, or used on its own or with a little butter as a dressing for pasta.

Balsamic vinegar (aceto balsamico)
Balsamic vinegar is the king of vinegars and is made in the area around Modena in Italy. It is the boiled and concentrated juice of local trebbiano grapes, which is aged over a very long period to give it a slightly syrupy texture and a rich, deep mahogany colour.

Index